Margaret Cooling is the author of over 50 books on RE and assem books for churches. For many years her speciality has been in us communicate Christianity within the field of education. She has number of publishers on this, including the National Gallery Company and the BBC. Margaret has taught in both primary and secondary schools and, for the last 25 years, has been engaged in writing and training across the UK. She trains both teachers and clergy to work in schools. In the past few years, Margaret has begun to adapt her experience and knowledge within the field of education to work with churches. Margaret has published two books for Barnabas: *Creating a Learning Church* (2005) and *Bible Storybags®* (2008).

Important information

Photocopy permission

The Copyright Licensing Agency (CLA)

Barnabas
in
Schools

Text copyright © Margaret Cooling 2012
Illustrations copyright © Ann Kronheimer 2012
The author asserts the moral right
to be identified as the author of this work

Published by
The Bible Reading Fellowship
15 The Chambers, Vineyard
Abingdon OX14 3FE
United Kingdom
Tel: +44 (0)1865 319700
Email: enquiries@brf.org.uk
Website: www.brf.org.uk
BRF is a Registered Charity

ISBN 978 1 84101 836 2

First published 2012
10 9 8 7 6 5 4 3 2 1 0

Acknowledgments
Unless otherwise stated, scripture quotations are taken from the Contemporary English Version of the Bible published by HarperCollins Publishers, copyright © 1991, 1992, 1995 American Bible Society.

The paper used in the production of this publication was supplied by mills that source their raw materials from sustainably managed forests. Soy-based inks were used in its printing and the laminate film is biodegradable.

A catalogue record for this book is available from the British Library

Printed in Singapore by Craft Print International Ltd

More Bible Storybags®

Reflective storytelling for primary
RE and assemblies

Margaret Cooling

To Charlotte and Isaac, who like stories

Acknowledgments

I would like to thank the following people for their help:

Doris Males for the knitting patterns and Rosa Davies for testing them

Althea Smith

Karen Turner and Ravenshead Church of England Primary School, Nottinghamshire, with thanks to class 1BM and Year 2

Sarah Holtom and Benhall Infant School, Cheltenham, Gloucestershire

Debbie Mobley and St Marks Church of England Junior School, Cheltenham, Gloucestershire

Contents

The scripts

Foreword

Good stories have layers of meaning that reveal themselves sometimes over a long period of time. This is especially true of Bible stories. For those getting to know the stories for the first time, help is needed to peel back the layers. As someone who has read stories from the Bible for my own benefit as well as in my role as educator for many years, I know that these stories have new treasures to be unearthed with each reading. I also admit to my ability to become immune to or blasé about the new treasures in stories. I can trick myself into thinking I know them fully. For this reason, I am indebted to Margaret Cooling who, over the years, has kept on producing resources for teachers to help children explore Bible stories.

More Bible Storybags® offers a multifaceted approach that helps both children and their teachers to get to know many Old Testament Bible stories well. Indeed, its elder sibling, *Bible Storybags®,* was eagerly bought by many of the schools I work with. This has resulted in pupils engaging with Bible stories from the New Testament in thoughtful, imaginative and creative ways. It has also involved members of some school communities getting their knitting needles out! Thereby a real enjoyment and ownership of the stories has been shared beyond the school gate.

Often, teachers lack confidence in teaching about Christianity within RE, and the more support they can get, the better. *More Bible Storybags®* gives ample information to help teachers feel confident in tackling a range of stories and unpacking their meanings in such an open, non-prescriptive way that the learning from the stories is entirely appropriate to the age and ability of each child. It provides tools to help children understand, play with and respond to the treasures and challenges contained within the Old Testament.

Although the stories have been written as scripts, they still contain the mystery, beauty and symbolism found in the original stories. Children are encouraged to bring all their natural intuition and curiosity to their encounter with them.

This book is a gem and I am happy to commend it.

Alison Brown, Deputy Director of Education and Schools Adviser, Diocese of Derby

Introduction

The scripts in this book can be used in RE or 'assembly' (Collective Worship/Religious Observance). In an assembly context, use a table so that all can see. Make sure you lift items high before placing them on the cloth. PowerPoint visuals of the story cloths are available for use alongside the bags for large venues (see www.barnabasinschools.org.uk/cooling2).

The book uses methods designed to stimulate both thinking and feeling—the creative and the cognitive. To this end, activities are provided for both creative arts and thinking skills.

In the scripts, meaning is conveyed by the rhythm of the language, the gestures, the objects and many 'cues' that the mind picks up intuitively. By the end of a story, pupils might feel they have come to some understanding without being able to put it into words. The biblical story and follow-up work often clarify what has been grasped intuitively. With this approach there is room for the pupils' ideas concerning the meaning of the stories, and for sharing the Christian community's understandings with the pupils.

The colour of the storybag® and many of the objects used are symbolic. For example, the cord in the story of Ruth represents friendship and commitment. Teachers can follow up these symbols or leave them without comment, depending on the age and aptitude of the pupils. British Sign Language is also used. A brief written description is given in the symbols section but teachers are recommended to watch the signs demonstrated on the websites provided.

Learning about and from religion: prayer and reflection

The approach used in this book enables pupils to learn about the Bible and learn from it. It encourages both a reflective and questioning response. Optional prayers are supplied for assemblies, and reflective activities are provided for RE for teachers to use as appropriate. Pupils can be invited to participate in reflections but should not feel that they have to. It is important that 'learning from' activities and reflections should not be intrusive.

Access for all

There are two scripts for each story, one suitable for younger pupils (4–7s) and one suitable for older pupils (7–11s), although teachers of lower junior pupils may wish to use the infant script. The scripts can be used in faith-based schools and community schools. Teachers will need to select from the follow-up material according to the age and ability of their pupils.

The methods used in this book give access to pupils of all abilities, as different ways of knowing are used (intuitive, symbolic, reasoning and so on). The scripts have been designed so that pupils can learn at different levels; the meanings are layered so that gifted and talented pupils can dig deeper into the symbolism and ideas.

Introducing and sharing Bible stories

Christian understandings of biblical stories can be shared with pupils using a form of words that earth the stories in the Christian tradition. For example, 'Today we are having a story that is important for Christians' or 'Today's story comes from the sacred book of the Christians, the Bible.' This leaves the pupil free to identify with the story or not. They can respond with 'That's my story; we read that at home / in my church' or 'Now I know why that is important for Christians.' It is important that pupils feel free to make their own response to the story, as long as it is respectful.

The scripts are deliberately ambiguous and relate to a biblical story without being that story. This stimulates curiosity—the basis for learning. They are designed to create conversation, encouraging the pupils to share their own ideas and ask questions. Pupils can become 'RE detectives' in order to work out who the characters are, what the script is about and how it relates to the biblical text. Packages such as 'WordArt' can be used to create badges or you can photocopy the templates overleaf.

I'm an RE Detective

The material in this book draws on insights from many areas: storysacks®, thinking skills, brain-based learning, Christian spirituality, Godly Play, the use of the creative arts, spiritual development and faith development. Each script is, however, original.

Symbolism and word images

Often, word images will be used to stimulate thinking. For example, life is likened to a chocolate box from which we have to choose; kindness is likened to a web, and enemies to animals of prey. These images can be explored with pupils with improvised drama to communicate the meaning.

Websites

Some websites are indicated for extra information or images. The websites do not necessarily reflect the views of the author of *More Bible Storybags*®. NB: Please check copyright on all websites before downloading any material.

I'm an RE Detective

Health and safety

All activities should be carried out with due regard to health and safety. Teachers are referred to their health and safety document. If any type of food is suggested within an activity, check for allergies and provide alternatives.

Pastoral issues

Sometimes Bible stories raise pastoral issues. For example, the stories of Ruth and Moses deal with death. Teachers are advised to bear in mind the age and maturity of their class when selecting material and be aware of any pastoral issues raised that may need following up.

Using the storybags® in RE and assembly

Select a storybag® script appropriate for the age of your pupils. Teachers of pupils aged 7–9 can use the script for younger or older pupils, depending on ability. You can either use the storybag® script followed by a few questions and then tell the biblical story, or tell the biblical story and then use the storybag® script as a way of reinforcing it or as a reflection.

An RE session using the bags can be organised in one of the following ways.

✿ One person can read the script while another person uses the bag.
✿ The script can be read as it is or used as a framework for the teacher to create his or her own retelling of the biblical story.
✿ The script can be recorded and played while the teacher uses the bag.

When you are ready to use the script, start by showing the bag and asking questions, such as these.

✿ Why do you think my bag is colourful?
✿ What sort of story might be in this bag?
✿ Does it remind you of anything?
✿ What do you think is in my bag?

Once you have done this, move to 'Unpacking the bag'. Choose from the following two approaches: a) is more of a presentation; b) is more interactive.

a) Read the 'Unpacking the bag' verse while the pupils listen. Take the items from the bag one at a time as they are mentioned. Lift them high so that all can see, then place them on the table or carpet in front of you, ready to use.
b) Ask questions as you take items from the bag and ask the pupils to help you to unpack.
   • What do you think this is?
   • Have you seen one of these before?

When pupils have offered their suggestions, read the 'Unpacking the bag' verse, lifting things up as they are mentioned and placing them ready to use.

> **Tips**
> ✳ Remember to pack the bag in reverse order—with items at the bottom if they are to come out last, and at the top if they are to come out first.
> ✳ Keep small items such as 'tears' in labelled envelopes with one glued to the outside, or in zipped transparent bags, whichever is appropriate for the age group.

Ways of telling the story

The 'cloth' is the bag laid flat on the carpet or table. It becomes the arena on which the story is played out. There are suggested actions to use with the scripts, but you can create your own as long as they are appropriate. Whatever actions are used, they should be unhurried and expressive.

Again, there are two approaches you can use; one is more participative than the other.

a) Presentation followed by participation: read the script as a presentation, waiting until the end for questions and participation.
b) Interactive throughout: ask questions as the story unfolds; encourage children to take part in moving figures and creating sound effects, joining in signs. For example, say, 'I wonder how the king feels now' or 'Could we make wave movements?'

Choose the style that suits you and adjust the scripts accordingly. Both styles have their merits. Sometimes a presentation without participation can build an atmosphere and have impact. At other times, interaction can make the story feel 'owned' by the pupils.

When you have finished the story script, you might want to choose a few questions from those listed at the end of the script or from page 11.

Making their own stories

Pupils can make their own stories that are not the biblical story. For example, you could say: 'We have a bag, a fish, a worm, a boat and some people. What stories could we make with these items?' You could go on to ask some of the following questions depending on the age of the pupils.

- ✪ What is the message of our story?
- ✪ Can we make different stories with the same 'ingredients'?
- ✪ Which story makes the most sense of the items?
- ✪ What criteria could we use to decide on the 'best' story using these objects?
- ✪ What would we mean by 'best'? Would it be the most exciting, the happiest or the one with the most helpful message?

Pupils look at the message of their own stories, then experience a presentation of the biblical story. What is the message of the biblical story? What makes the biblical story different from their story or other stories with the same 'ingredients'? Interview someone who is a Christian about what makes the biblical stories authoritative for them. NB: Do not use this method with very sensitive stories.

Using the PowerPoint slides

Go to the website www.barnabasinschools.org.uk/cooling2. Select the PowerPoint you want from the menu and follow the instructions.

You can use the bag and the PowerPoint slides together if you are in a large venue. Make sure all your actions are large and you hold items up high. The PowerPoint slides will make sure the pupils see what they need to follow the story.

RE thinking skills and follow-up work

A 'thinking skills' approach

The scripts can be used for thinking skills in RE across the age groups. You might like to use the 'detective badge' idea on page 8 as part of this approach.

KS2 / P4–7 (7–11 years)

After the presentation, use the initial questions to stimulate thinking. Suggested questions are as follows:

- What is interesting about this story?
- What is puzzling or surprising?
- What did you like?
- What did you dislike?
- Does this story have a message or meaning? What is it?

Ask pupils to formulate questions about the script. You may want to repeat the presentation, asking pupils to think of the questions they want to ask. They should be questions that concentrate on meaning, ideas and feelings and cannot be easily answered from the text. Write up the questions, grouping related questions together. For example, some may all be about right and wrong. Select a question or group of questions to discuss.

Introduce the biblical story that goes with the script as a way of responding to the questions. The biblical story should add to the discussion, not close it down. Explore how the story and the script might interact. Does the biblical story help us to understand the script? Does the script help us to understand the biblical story?

Reflect on what pupils have learned from their discussion. Encourage them to express what they have understood in forms such as writing, art and dance.

KS1 / P2–3 (5–7 years)

Younger pupils can watch a presentation, after which the teacher creates questions as follows.

- Questions about feelings: 'Who in the story feels sad? I wonder why that is.'
- Questions about thinking: 'I wonder what the brothers are thinking.'
- Questions about speech: 'I wonder what the women are saying to each other.'
- Questions about behaviour: 'Why did he stop and look?'
- Questions about meaning: 'What is this story all about?'
- Questions about symbols: 'I wonder why the bag has lots of lines.'

The questions can be asked using the figures from the bags, role play and drawings of faces showing different emotions. Wherever possible, reduce abstract questioning.

This section draws on the work of Robert Fisher and others. For more information, go to: www.teachingthinking.net.

Follow-up work

The following activities can be used with every script. Select according to the age and aptitude of your pupils and the time you have available.

Discuss with pupils the following initial questions.

- The significance of colours, including the colour of the bag.
- Their feelings about the story script: do different parts of the story make them feel differently? How do characters feel at different moments?
- Who do they think the characters in the script are?
- What do they think is the most important moment in the story and why?
- The meaning of the story script: does it have anything to say to us?

Select from the following activities.

- Pupils can retell the story to themselves, using their own language and the items from the bag. Make sure everything is safe, replacing items as necessary. If a drawstring is used on the bag, you can remove this for young children. Pupils can make their own story bag or story shoebox using simple and safe materials.
- Explore the relationship between the text and the story. Use the biblical story to unlock the meaning of the script. Use the script to help children understand the meaning of the biblical story.
- Pupils might like to hear the story again or read a book that is based on the story.
- Does the title help us to understand the story? Can the pupils think of a better title?
- Pupils can express their ideas in art, creating images for parts of a story.
- Use a script for thinking skills (see page 11).
- Give children some new words for feelings. Move the characters about and remind them of how people felt and why.
- Older pupils might like to write their own script in this format.
- Do they think the author has got it right? Are there places where they would change things?
- Why do they think Christians still read this story?

Plain script

A plain script can be created by photocopying the script and blocking out the actions and the 'Unpacking' section. Use this as a photocopy master for activities requiring a plain script.

Using the scripts with older pupils

Older pupils might like to try some of the following.

- The PowerPoint version.
- Demonstrate the method using a bag and figures, and then ask pupils to create their own script and sack for younger pupils, using a plain script and adding their own actions. Shoeboxes covered in giftwrap can replace sacks. Make sure all items are safe for the intended age group.
- Pupils can create their own PowerPoint presentation of the script by using a digital camera, taking photographs of a presentation at key points.
- Create a drama or dance from the script, using pupils rather than figures.
- Pupils can annotate the plain script for reading aloud, preparing it for presentation.
- Turn a script into a book. How will pupils divide the text? How will they illustrate it?

Creating the storybags®

Fabric bags are simple to make. Alternatively, you can use coloured paper bags. Shoeboxes covered in coloured paper could also be used, but you would need to adjust the wording of the scripts slightly and add a cloth to the box in the appropriate colour.

To make a bag, take half a metre of fabric, about 115–122cm in width. Fold the fabric in half, right sides together, and sew down the longer sides (see figure 1).

To make a hem, turn over the top 1cm and iron in place, then turn over another 3cm and iron in place. Machine round this hem, leaving a 2cm gap. Fasten off securely (see figure 2).

Thread 1.5m of ribbon through the hem, entering and leaving by the small gap. Tie the ends of the ribbon to stop them being pulled through (see figure 3).

Turn the bag right-side-out to finish.

NB: Omit the ribbon if the bag is to be used by small children, or use shoeboxes instead of bags.

> Teachers may wish to create a giant Bible storybag® with different images of Bible stories on the front, to show that all the separate stories make one large story (see figure 4).

Finding the objects

The objects suggested in the scripts are often available in the classroom. Playmobil® people or something similar can be used for the characters in the scripts. Easy patterns for knitted people are provided on pages 14–15.

> All items used must be safe for the intended age group and ability of the children.

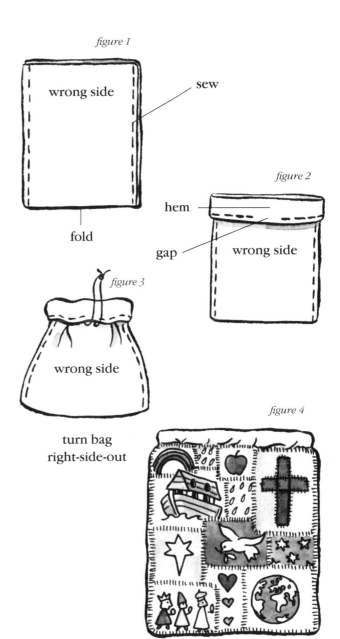

figure 1

wrong side

sew

fold

figure 2

hem

gap

wrong side

figure 3

wrong side

turn bag
right-side-out

figure 4

Pattern for knitted people

The basic figure

This is a basic figure, knitted in stocking stitch (see diagram 1).

- ✪ For a standard size figure, ignore the numbers in brackets.
- ✪ For a large figure (Goliath) replace the standard numbers with those in brackets.
- ✪ For a small figure (child-size David or Esther) knit the standard size figure on size 12 (2.75mm) needles, using 4-ply wool. You can also take four rows off the height by knitting five rows on the * instruction rather than nine. When making up the figure, make the circle of card 4cm in diameter rather than 5cm and reduce the size of the opening on the base to 2cm rather than 2.5cm.

✂ You will need
- ✳ Double knitting yarn in small amounts: body colour, face colour and hair colour
- ✳ 1 pair of size 10 knitting needles (3.25mm)
- ✳ Stuffing that conforms to health and safety regulations
- ✳ Large-eyed sewing needle

Vary the body colours to differentiate the figures. For example, make an army all one colour or friends a particular colour.

Body

Cast on 26 (30) stitches in body colour.
Knit 1, make 1 in the next stitch; repeat to the end of the row. You should have 39 (45) stitches by the end of this first row.
*Beginning with a purl row, stocking stitch for 9 (11) rows.

diagram 1

Knit 8 (10) stitches, knit 2 together, knit 19 (21), knit 2 together, knit 8 (10).
Knit stocking stitch for 5 (7) rows.
Knit 8 (10) stitches, knit 2 together, knit 17 (19), knit 2 together, knit 8 (10).
Knit stocking stitch for 5 (7) rows.
Knit 8 (10) stitches, knit 2 together, knit 15 (17), knit 2 together, knit 8 (10).
Knit stocking stitch for 3 (5) rows.
Knit 8 (10) stitches, knit 2 together, knit 13 (15), knit 2 together, knit 8 (10).
Stocking stitch for 4 (6) rows. Change to face colour.
Purl 2 together to the end of the row.
Stocking stitch for 2 rows.
Knit 2 together, knit to last 2 stitches, knit 2 together.
Knit 4 (6), make 1 in the next 2 stitches, knit to the last 6 (8) stitches, make 1 in the next 2 stitches, knit 4 (6) stitches.
Stocking stitch for 6 (7) rows.
Starting with a purl row, stocking stitch next 3 rows in hair colour. Break the yarn, leaving a long end.
Thread the yarn through remaining stitches and pull up.

Arms

Cast on 12 (16) stitches in body colour.

Knit 14 (16) rows of stocking stitch.

Change to face colour, knit 4 rows. Break the yarn, leaving a long end.

Thread the yarn through the stitches, pull up and then sew up the seam to create a tube.

Sewing up

Starting at the head, sew up the seam in the matching colour. Sew down approximately 2.5cm on to the body area.

Thread a piece of yarn through the base of the body and pull it up until you have a circular opening approximately 2.5cm in diameter.

Sew up the back seam to approximately 2.5cm from the base. You should now have a tube with a gap in the middle of the seam.

Cut 2–3 circles of thick card, 5 or 6cm in diameter. (2–3 thicknesses of card from a writing pad work well.) Push the card through the gap and press it down into the base. This will help the figure to stand.

Push the stuffing through the gap and up into the head and body. This will keep the card in place and stiffen the figure (see diagram 2).

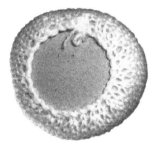

diagram 2

Sew up the back seam using matching yarn. Run a few stitches around the neck part of the figure, pull and fasten off to create a neck.

Sew up the arms, leaving an opening at the top. Stuff the arms and sew to the sides of the figure.

Using embroidery cotton or wool, embroider two eyes and a mouth if you wish, or leave the face blank so that pupils can imagine the expression.

Alternative simple pattern for figures

The pattern below can be used for simple figures that require no stuffing. They are easy to knit and can be made to stand by inserting paper cups inside. They can also be used as hand puppets.

To vary the size of these puppets, just reduce or enlarge the number of centimetres of stocking stitch at the * instruction. For Goliath knit 9cm, and for David and Esther knit 5cm of stocking stitch. Differentiate the figures by colour and by adding crowns for kings and queens.

 You will need
* Double knitting yarn in small amounts: body colour, face colour, hair colour
* 1 pair of size 10 knitting needles (3.25mm)
* Large-eyed sewing needle

Cast on 40 stitches and knit 3 rows plain.

* Starting with a plain row, knit 7cm of stocking stitch.

Break off the wool and join on the face colour.

Stocking stitch 4cm, ending with a purl row.

Break off the wool and join on the hair colour.

Stocking stitch for 2 rows, ending with a purl row.

Knit 2 together all along the row.

Break off the wool, leaving a fairly long end.

Thread the wool through a sewing needle. Thread the sewing needle through the stitches on the knitting needle and lift them off (they will now be on the sewing needle). Pull the sewing needle through so that the stitches are on the wool thread.

Pull very slightly (do not bunch: the face needs to be flat).

Wrong side: sew across the top of the head and down the back.

Right side: add French knots for eyes, using embroidery silk.

Use a single line for the mouth with a stitch in the centre to give it shape and to secure it.

Male headdress for puppets

Cast on 32 stitches.

Knit three rows of garter stitch (plain).

* Knit 2 together, knit to the end of the row, knit 2 together.

* Knit all along next row.

Repeat * rows until all the stitches have gone.

Thread wool through last stitch. Stitch on to head (see diagram 3).

diagram 3

Female headdress

As above, but knit a larger triangle and use stocking stitch, or knit a rectangle and gather along the top.

Knitted crown for king or queen puppets

Cast on 22 stitches (use glitter wool if available).
Knit 2–3 rows of garter stitch (plain).
Cast off. Sew into a circle.
Stitch on to the head (see diagram 4). Decorate.

diagram 4

Decorating puppets

☻ Inserts can be knitted and sewn on the front of the puppets.
☻ Braid can be used.
☻ The first three rows of plain can be a different colour.

Knitting pattern for a baby

> ✂ **You will need**
> ✱ Double knitting yarn
> ✱ 1 pair of size 10 knitting needles (3.25mm)
> ✱ Large-eyed sewing needle
> ✱ Stuffing that conforms to health and safety regulations

Cast on 8 stitches.
Knit stocking stitch for 11 rows.
Row 12: purl 2 together, purl to last 2 stitches, purl 2 together.
Cut the wool, leaving a long end.

Thread the long piece of wool through a large-eyed sewing needle and thread it through the stitches on the knitting needle, lifting each one as you do so.
Pull the thread to gather this end. Do not cut the thread.
Form the knitting into a tube (longest edges together), wrong side out.
Starting at the gathered end (this will be the head), sew the edges together, using the long thread and taking small stitches.
Turn right-side-out. Add stuffing.
Run the thread around the bottom end, gather and pull up. Do not cut the thread. The figure should now look like a sausage.
Push the needle in the bottom of the back seam and bring it out about two-thirds of the way down. Oversew on the spot with two small stitches to secure the thread. Run a gathering thread around the tube and pull to create a head.
Wind the wool around the 'neck' once and fasten off at the back.
Cut a tiny triangle of cloth for a shawl or use the knitted blanket below.

Knitting pattern for Moses basket

> ✂ **You will need**
> ✱ Double knitting yarn (used double throughout)
> ✱ 1 pair of size 10 knitting needles (3.25mm)

Use plain stitch throughout.
Cast on 14 stitches, knit 8 rows.
Cast on 5 stitches at the beginning of the next 2 rows.
Knit 8 rows.
Cast off 5 stitches at the beginning of the next 2 rows.
Knit 8 rows, cast off. Sew corners together to form basket.

Knitting pattern for lining or 'mattress'

> ✂ **You will need**
> ✱ Double knitting yarn
> ✱ 1 pair of size 10 knitting needles (3.25mm)

Use stocking stitch throughout.
Cast on 22 stitches, knit 22 rows, cast off.
Fold in half with the two edges underneath (see diagram 5).
Sew into the inside of the basket.

Edges meet on the underside　　　　*diagram 5*

The finished Moses basket

Knitting pattern for a blanket

✂ You will need
* Double knitting yarn
* 1 pair of size 8 needles (4mm)

Use stocking stitch throughout.
Cast on 14 stitches, knit 12 rows.
Cast off and steam press.

Knitting pattern for sheep

✂ You will need
* Double knitting yarn
* 1 pair of size 10 knitting needles (3.25mm)
* Stuffing that conforms to health and safety regulations
* Large-eyed sewing needle

NB: Each time you cast on, leave a long end, as you will need it.

Body

Cast on 9 stitches, knit 12 rows in stocking stitch.
Knit 2 together, knit to the last 2 stitches, knit 2 together (this will leave you 7 stitches).

Cut the wool, leaving a long end.
Thread the long piece of wool through a large-eyed sewing needle and thread it through the 7 stitches on the knitting needle, lifting each one off as you do so.
Pull the thread to gather this end (to form the head).
Turn the knitting so that the purl side (bumpy side) is on the outside and sew up the seam to form a tube.
Leave the other end (tail end) open and add stuffing until firm. Sew up the tail end and fasten off.

Head

Cast on 7 stitches, knit 5 rows of stocking stitch.
Knit 2 together 3 times, then knit 1.
Cut the wool and leave a long end, then thread the wool through the stitches on the needle as before.
Pull up tight to form the sheep's face and then sew along the seam of the tiny tube, leaving the other end (neck end) open.
Stuff the tube lightly and sew up the back seam (neck end).
Sew the head on to the body (make sure you sew it to the head end).

Ears (x 2)

Cast on two stitches, knit one row.
Cut the wool, leaving a long end, and thread it back through the stitches as before.
Take the two ends and tie into a knot. Sew to the head.

Legs (x 4)

Cast on 3 stitches, knit 3 rows.
Cut the wool, leaving a long end, and thread it back through the stitches as before.
Tie the two ends tightly and sew into place (they should be ball shaped).

Tail

Tie a knot in the centre of a double length of wool (30cm long before doubling).
Cut the wool about 1 cm below the knot and fringe it to form a tail.
Use the long ends to sew the tail to the body with the knot.

The scripts

In the beginning

Creation

Using the storybag® in assembly

You will need
* Some apples
* Two boxes, one labelled 'Good', the other labelled 'Rubbish'

Introduce the assembly by setting up a sorting scenario in which two pupils stand at a table sorting apples into good and bad. For example, they might say, 'Not too many bad apples today.'

Say, 'Today's story is about our world. Listen carefully for the word "good". How many times is it used?' Tell the Bible story (see page 21). Alternatively, use an internet version of the story. For example:

* www.refuel.org.uk/projects/ks1_topics/old_testament/old_testament.html (for an online turn-the-page audiovisual of the creation story)
* www.jesusandkidz.com/html/j_gen_00.htm (online slides)

Comment

Throughout the Bible story of creation, God keeps saying 'Good' or 'Very good'. Unlike our apple sorters, God did not find anything bad, because God doesn't make rubbish. God gave our world a big 'thumbs up'.

Reflection

Use the storybag® script 1 or 2 as a reflection. It can be read by the teacher, with pupils performing any gestures, sign language or sounds. Pupils can also hold up objects and people from the bag. PowerPoint visuals of the story cloths can be accessed via www.barnabasinschools.org.uk/cooling2.

Prayer (*optional*)

God, your smile warms our world and we know you love what you have made. Help us to love it, too.

Using the storybag® in RE

Introduce the subject using some of the material from the assembly introduction (see page 20). On the same page you will find a comment on the biblical story.

Select the appropriate script and turn to pages 9 and 10 to find ways of using it.

Biblical material

Genesis 1:1—2:3

In the beginning, the earth was just a great big empty nothing, a watery soup of darkness, but God was there. God said, 'Let there be light!' And there was. 'Good!' said God. God split light from dark. He called the light 'day' and the darkness 'night'. That was the first day.

God said, 'Let the waters be divided by the sky! Let there be rain in the sky above and water on the earth below.' And that's what happened. That was the second day.

God said, 'Let the waters that are on the earth come together to make seas, so that there is dry land.' And it happened! The seas came together and dry ground appeared. God called the dry ground 'land'. Then God said, 'Let the land be covered with plants and trees with fruit.' And plants turned the land from brown to green. 'Good!' said God. That was the third day.

God said, 'Let there be lights in the sky to give light and dark.' And God made the sun, moon and stars to hang in the sky.' 'Good!' said God. That was the fourth day.

God said, 'Let the seas be full of all things that swim, and let birds fill the air.' And it was so. God saw that they were good and blessed them and said, 'Fill my world, both sea and sky.' That was the fifth day.

God said, 'Let the land be full of living things of every kind, wild and tame animals.' And it was so. Then God made people, a little like himself. He gave them a world to be responsible for and placed it in their care. God blessed them and said, 'Fill my world and take charge of it.' And God saw that all he had made was very good. That was the sixth day.

On the seventh day, God rested, because he had finished making the world. He blessed this day and made it holy.

Follow-up activities

Select from the activities below, according to the age and aptitude of your pupils. (See also pages 11 and 12.)

1. Create a wall display of this story that reflects the layout of the bag. Add two-dimensional versions of items from the story. Sections of the script can act as captions. Add pupils' questions and comments, and use them as a basis for discussion. Place the appropriate story script and an open children's Bible on a table. Add to the table things the pupils have created and descriptions of how they feel about their creations.

2. Make a simple creation jigsaw puzzle. Cut an A3 thick sheet of paper or card into four strips, lengthways. Using one strip, divide it into seven sections. Cut each of the seven sections with a simple jigsaw connection. Pupils can retell the story using the pieces, adding pictures and text. Important beliefs can be written on the back (see background information on page 22). The jigsaws can be muddled and reassembled in the correct order.

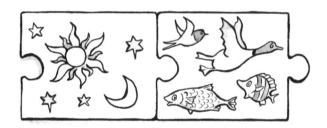

3. Make crowns and add words, on paper jewel shapes, that are important to understanding the Christian idea of looking after the earth for God and being responsible for it. (The background information on page 22 includes an explanation of this belief.) As a class, collect words and phrases to use in sentences to explain the crowns—for example, 'care', 'look after', 'serve' and 'rule'. Older pupils can use the thesaurus for this task.

4. Pupils can create a reflective PowerPoint slideshow for the story of creation, using a series of images and their own commentary. See the 'Useful websites' section on page 22 for copyright-friendly sites. Alternatively, together as a class, create your own commentary to the slideshow on the website www. jesusandkidz.com/html/j_gen_00.htm.

5. As a class or individually, make up a blessing for the world. What are the good things we want for our world? Work through the different parts of creation

and think of a blessing for each part. Print the blessing on coloured paper, roll and tie with ribbon. Add to the display in such a way that the roll can be untied and read.

An example of a blessing might be:

May your forests grow tall,
May your rivers run full,
May your animals run free…

Older pupils may wish to form the blessing into a poem by adjusting the rhythm.

6. Find out about the work of A Rocha UK, a Christian environmental agency. Create a profile of this organisation. See the website www.arocha.org/int-en/work.html (teacher support is needed).

Symbols used in the story

⚙ The word: this is a symbol of God's power (he just says it and it is done). Jesus is also described as the Word (see John 1:1–3).

Signs used in the story (British Sign Language)

⚙ 'No': hand waved back and forth across face.
⚙ 'God': right hand at shoulder level, right index finger points upward, other digits curled inwards.

Useful websites

⚙ www.signstation.org (go to the BSL dictionary, then A–Z for the word 'no')
⚙ www.christiansigns.org.uk (search 'vocab' for the word 'God')
⚙ www.britishsignlanguage.com

Reflective activity

Show some pupils' slideshows of creation (see activity 4 on page 21).

Alternatively, use www.jesusandkidz.com (select Bible stories > God's wonderful world). Play the sequence without sound.

Ask pupils to think about the part of creation that they regard as the 'best gift'.

Assessment

Assess the pupils' understanding by observing them replaying the script, or ask them to talk about the display or write about it.

Background information and understanding the story

⚙ Christians believe that God created the world; it did not just happen by chance. For Christians, the intricate design in creation points to a Creator. Christians understand this Bible story in different ways: some take it as literal truth, while others would see it as spiritual truth told in a way appropriate for its time. Believing in a Creator God does not preclude Christians from being scientists. Explore the website www.scibel.com for more information.

⚙ The Christian doctrine of the Trinity puts the emphasis on relationship at the heart of the Godhead: Father, Son and Holy Spirit. Christians believe that this relationship means that God did not create because he was lonely; he created because he wanted to do so.

⚙ The Bible talks of people being made in God's image. This does not mean that people look like God; it means that they reflect some aspects of God in the way they are made—for example, the ability to love, make relationships, create and think. It also means that people should reflect God to the world in the way they behave.

⚙ The Bible sees the world as belonging to God and on loan to people, who are given authority to rule the earth. This does not mean that they may dominate or exploit it. 'Rule' in the Bible only ever means 'rule under God'. Jesus showed what a ruler should be like: he was a king who served others. The authority given to humanity is to bring creative order and to be 'servant kings'. To communicate this idea, a phrase about caring for the earth has been added to the Bible story.

⚙ A blessing is the good that God or others want for someone. A traditional blessing from the Bible is 'May God bless you and keep you. May God shine his face upon you and give you his peace' (Numbers 6:24–25, paraphrased).

⚙ Christians believe that God the Father, Jesus and the Holy Spirit were all involved in creation. John 1:1 talks of Jesus as the Word, being with God at the beginning.

Useful websites

⚙ www.photolib.noaa.gov/about.html (for images)
⚙ www.textweek.com/art/creation.htm
(select scripture index for other information)
⚙ www.refuel.org.uk/projects/ks1_topics/old_testament/old_testament.html
⚙ www.bibleforchildren.org/languages/english/stories.php (01: When God made everything)

Script 1

Unpacking the bag

My bag is dark, but there are colours in my bag:
silver, blue and brown of the earth.
There is rain in my bag that falls from above
to water plants on the earth below.
There are lights in my bag: sun, moon and stars.
There are creatures in my bag:
fish and birds and animals that walk the land.
There are people in my bag: called to care.

The story

In the beginning was nothing, nothing at all *(place bag)*: no trees and no flowers *(shake head, sign 'no')*, no animals and no people *(sign 'no', shake head)*. All was dark. All was silent *(finger on lip)* but the Spirit of God was there *(undulate hand over the bag)*.

God said, 'Light!' and the darkness ended *(place silver over the bag)*. God gathered light together to make day, and he gathered dark together to make night *(gather silver to one side and dark blue bag to other side with a gap the size of the bag in the middle)*. 'Good!' said God, and that was Day One *(show one finger)*.

God made sky to divide the waters of the earth *(place pale blue cloth in the gap)*: rain in the sky above, sea below *(sprinkle raindrops on top half of pale blue cloth; children make rain sounds)*. And that was Day Two *(show two fingers)*.

God brought the waters on the earth together to make seas *(bunch up bottom of blue cloth into a narrow wavy band)*, and land appeared *(place brown cloth beneath blue cloth)*. God made plants that turned the land green *(scatter bushes on brown cloth)*. 'Good!' said God, and that was Day Three *(show three fingers)*.

God hung the sun, moon and stars in the sky to give lights for day and night *(add sun to pale blue cloth; add moon and stars to dark blue cloth)*. 'Good!' said God, and that was Day Four *(show four fingers)*.

God filled the seas with all that swims *(add fish to bottom of pale blue cloth; put hands together and wiggle like a fish)*. He filled the sky with all that flies *(add birds to top of pale blue cloth; cross wrists to make flying movement)*. 'Good!' said God, and that was Day Five *(show five fingers)*.

After that, God filled the land with animals of every sort: wild and woolly, slow and speedy *(add animals to brown cloth)*. Finally, God added people *(add people to brown cloth)* and gave them the world to care for. 'Good!' said God. 'Very good!' And that was Day Six *(show six fingers)*.

On the last day, God rested, and that was Day Seven *(show seven fingers)*.

Reproduced with permission from *More Bible Storybags*® published by BRF 2012 (978 1 84101 836 2) www.barnabasinschools.org.uk

You will need
* A dark blue bag
* Silver fabric (same size as the bag)
* Brown cloth (half size of the bag)
* Pale blue cloth (same size as the bag)
* Silver paper raindrops and rainsticks, if you have them
* Sun, moon and stars made from card
* Tissue plants (bunched-up green tissue)
* Birds, fish, land animals (use class animal sets, pictures or felt cut-outs)
* Two people figures (one man, one woman)

Questions
(See also page 11.)
* Can there be nothing at all?
* Why does God say 'Good' and 'Very good'?
* Why do you think people and animals were made at the same time?
* Why is one day a rest day?

Older pupils

You will need

* A dark blue bag
* Silver fabric (same size as the bag)
* Brown cloth (half size of the bag)
* Two pale blue cloths (each half size of the bag, joined with tape)
* Silver paper raindrops (rainsticks if you have them)
* Sun, moon and stars made from card
* Tissue paper plants (bunched-up green tissue)
* Birds, fish, land animals (use class animal sets or pictures)
* Two people figures (one man, one woman)
* Label: 'To the world with love'
* Small piece of mirror card

Script 2

Unpacking the bag

My bag is dark, but there are colours in my bag:
silver, blue and earthy brown.
There is rain in my bag that falls from above
to water plants on the earth below.
There are lights in my bag: sun, moon and stars.
There are creatures in my bag:
fish and birds and animals that stalk the land.
There are people my bag: called to care.
There is a label in my bag, signed with love, and a mirror that reflects—
but what, we do not know.

The story

My bag is the shade of darkness, for in the beginning there was great darkness…	*Place bag and smooth it*
no light, no land, no place, no people.	*Sign 'no'*
And the Spirit moved across the deep.	*Undulate hand over the bag*
The Word spoke 'Light!'	*Place silver fabric over the bag*
And light filled the world.	
Light was gathered to form day…	*Gather silver to one side*
and the dark was gathered to form night.	*Gather dark to other side, leaving a sizable gap*
'Good!' A day ended. One.	*Hold up one finger*
The Word spoke 'Sky!'	*Hold up pale blue cloth*
And sky split the waters.	*Tear cloth apart*
Rain above the earth…	*Place one cloth at the top; add drops*
and waters that covered the earth.	*Place the other cloth underneath*
Another day ended. Two.	*Hold up two fingers*
The Word spoke 'Land!' and gathered the waters into seas.	*Bunch lower blue cloth into narrow sea*

Reproduced with permission from *More Bible Storybags*® published by BRF 2012 (978 1 84101 836 2) www.barnabasinschools.org.uk

IN THE BEGINNING (CREATION)

Dry land appeared.	*Place brown cloth under sea*
The Word willed life, and plants turned land from brown to green.	*Sprinkle plants*
'Good!' Another day. Three.	*Hold up three fingers*
The Word spoke 'Lights!' And the sun shone by day...	*Place sun in sky*
and moon and stars lit the night.	*Place moon and stars on the dark cloth*
'Good!' Another day. Four.	*Hold up four fingers*
The word spoke 'Life!' And the air filled with birds...	*Add birds to sky area*
and seas swarmed with fish...	*Add fish to sea*
great and glorious, small and sleek; all manner of life.	*Place hands together and move them like a fish*
'Good!' Another day. Five.	*Hold up five fingers*
The Word spoke 'Life!' once more, and animals roamed the earth...	*Scatter animals on land*
wild and wonderful...	*Make claws with fingers*
timid and tame.	*Move fingers like a running mouse*
Then the Word willed another being into life...	*Add people*
a small reflection of himself.	*Add mirror*
He gifted them the world...	*Add label*
theirs to enjoy, theirs to rule, theirs to care.	
'Very good!' Another day. Six.	*Hold up six fingers*
Then there was silence and not a word was spoken.	*Finger on lips*
A silent blessing spread across the world.	*Undulate hands over the world*
'Shh.' Another day. Seven.	*Finger on lips. Hold up seven fingers*

Questions

(See also page 11.)

* Who is the Word?
* Why is 'Good' repeated?
* How would you finish the label?
* Why is one day quiet?
* How can people be a reflection of someone else?

Reproduced with permission from *More Bible Storybags®* published by BRF 2012 (978 1 84101 836 2) www.barnabasinschools.org.uk

IN THE BEGINNING (CREATION)

The testing tree

Adam and Eve make a choice

 You will need

* Sweets or fruit (check food allergies)

Introduce the assembly with a test that involves making a choice to obey. For example, sit a pupil (who is likely to succeed) in front of a plate of sweets or fruit and say that they must not eat any for one or two minutes. If they succeed in waiting, they can choose two sweets or fruits. You leave the room and come back after one or two minutes. (Other teachers should be in the room: pupils must not be unattended.) When you come back, ask the pupil if they have eaten any sweets or fruit. If they have not, they can choose two. Ask the pupil how difficult it was to wait. Ask the others if the pupil was free to choose to eat straight away or to wait.

Today's story is about choosing and obedience. Read the Bible story on page 27.

Comment

Adam and Eve were given everything they needed in the garden. They had a close friendship with God and only one rule. Adam and Eve were free to keep the rule or break it: God made them so that they could choose. By choosing to break the one rule, Adam and Eve spoilt their friendship with God.

Although Christians understand this story differently, they agree on its message. For Christians, this story is about people disobeying God and spoiling their friendship with him. It is about people being created with the freedom to make choices—good or bad—and spoiling the world by making wrong choices.

We have the same freedom as the people in the story did. We have the freedom to make choices, good or bad, but what we do affects others and also affects our world. People can choose to lie or steal, hurt others and be selfish. We can also choose to tell the truth, be honest, love and care for others.

Reflection

Use the storybag® script 1 or 2 as a reflection. It can be read by the teacher, with pupils performing any gestures, sign language or sounds. Pupils can also hold up objects and people from the bag. PowerPoint visuals of the story cloths can be accessed via www. barnabasinschools.org.uk/cooling2.

 Prayer (optional)

Father God, maker of all, you created us free to choose. Guide our choices and help us to choose what is right when we are tempted to make wrong choices.

Introduce the subject using some of the material from the assembly introduction (see page 26). On the same page you will find a comment on the biblical story. Select the appropriate script and turn to pages 9 and 10 to find ways of using it.

Biblical material

Genesis 2:15—3:14, 20–24

When the world was young, Adam and Eve lived in the garden called Eden, given to them by God. God told them to care for his garden and keep it in order. All was at peace in the garden; God, the people and the animals lived together in friendship. God told Adam and Eve that they could eat fruit from every tree except one. They must not eat the fruit of the tree that had the power to let them know fully the difference between right and wrong. God told them that great harm would come from eating that fruit.

Now the snake was a sneaky creature. He went to Eve and lied to her: he told her that the tree God had forbidden was harmless—she could eat the fruit and know as much as God. Eve wanted to be as clever as God, so she ate the fruit, and so did Adam. The first thing they noticed was that they had no clothes on. Before, they had been quite happy as they were. The next thing they noticed was the sound of God walking in the garden.

'Have you eaten that forbidden fruit?' said God.

'Eve told me to,' said Adam.

'The snake told me to,' said Eve.

The snake had no one else to blame and crept away under the anger of God. God looked with sadness at his new world. Already, lies, envy, deceit and disobedience had crept in; more would follow. The two people had made their choice, so they would have to live in a world spoilt by their decisions. God made clothes for them and they left the garden; life would be harder now, in a world spoilt by wrong. But that was not the end of the story. God had a plan.

Follow-up activities

Select from the activities below, according to the age and aptitude of your pupils. (See also pages 11 and 12.)

1. Create a wall display of this story that reflects the layout of the bag. Add two-dimensional versions of items from the story. Sections of the script can act as captions. Add pupils' questions and comments, and use them as a basis for discussion. Place the appropriate story script and an open children's Bible on a table.

2. Make a pop-up version of the story. Fold an A4 sheet of lightweight card in half widthways. Cut two slits. Fold the cut section the opposite way so that it stands out. Pupils can draw a tree to cut out and stick on the pop-up section. A retelling of the story and an explanation of why Christians read it can be written around the tree.

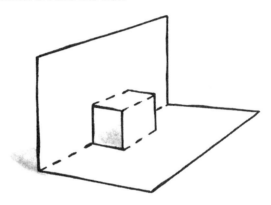

3. As a class, create a modern scenario in which people are tempted to do something wrong. This can be enacted as a drama. Locate points in the drama where people could act differently and enact different endings.

4. Explore how artists express Christian understandings of the story. Encourage pupils to express what they have learned, based on the style of a chosen artist. (See the 'Useful websites' section on page 28.)

5. This is a story about breaking a friendship with God rather than breaking a rule. The whole of the rest of the Bible is about mending the friendship with God. What sort of behaviour breaks our friendships with each other? How do we put things right? Enact some scenarios and photograph and caption them (with permission). Ask pupils what they think God's plan for mending the friendship was.

6. Discuss what biblical 'peace' means. (See the note on shalom in the background information on page 28.) Script 2 talks of peace radiating like the spokes of a wheel. Draw a wheel and, between the spokes, write or draw some of the things that would make our world peaceful. Around the wheel, write what 'shalom' means.

Symbols used in the story

- The tree of knowledge: a full knowledge of right and wrong, a test of obedience.
- The garden: a symbol of the world before it went wrong.
- The snake: a symbol of wrong.

Signs used in the story (British Sign Language)

- 'Sad': right hand held vertically in front of the face, side on. Move downward to just below the chin.
- 'Lie': right index finger drawn across mouth diagonally.
- 'Choice': right hand pointing to audience. Thumb and index finger pinch together, then open.
- 'God': right hand at shoulder level, right index finger points upward, other digits curled inwards.

Useful websites

- www.signstation.org (go to the BSL dictionary, then A–Z for the words 'lie' and 'choice')
- www.christiansigns.org.uk (search 'vocab' for the word 'God')
- www.britishsignlanguage.com (for the word 'sad')

Reflective activity

This story is about being free to choose. Give each pupil a piece of string with a loose knot in it. The knot is a symbol of a wrong choice. We hear of wrong choices on the news—for example, people stealing and hurting others. We experience wrong choices when people are nasty to us or we are nasty to them.

We cannot straighten out our world and get rid of the wrong choices as easily as undoing a knot. (Undo the knot.) We can, however, make better choices, and Christians believe that people can ask God's help to do this. (All run string through fingers as pupils think of one good choice they have made.)

Assessment

Assess the pupils' understanding by observing them replaying the script, or ask them to talk about the display or write about it.

Background information and understanding the story

- Christians understand this story in different ways: some see it as literal truth; others see it as spiritual truth. All would agree that the message of the story is that the world is not now as God intended.
- Adam means 'man' or 'humankind', and Eve means 'living'. The tree of knowledge symbolises a full knowledge of right and wrong.
- In Hebrew, the word for peace is 'shalom', which means that everything is fair, right and complete. It is about how people feel: restful, content and well. It is also about the way the world should be: just, without war, with right relationships between people and nations and the created world.
- The story of the testing tree is about free will. God puts Adam and Eve in a garden and gives them everything they could want and only one rule. They are free to break the rule or not, but they have to live with the consequences if they are to be genuine moral beings.
- Envy (wanting to be as wise as God), lies, deceit and disobedience are the beginning of humanity's use of freedom to choose in the wrong way. Not only do the people who make the decisions have to live with the consequences, but so do future generations. We suffer the results of our own and other people's wrong choices.
- The Bible talks of another tree in the garden: the tree that gave life. Adam and Eve leave the garden and the gate is closed behind them. The tree that gave life (immortality) is guarded.
- God had a plan: he did not give up on people. The Old Testament is the story of God entering into a relationship with various people and making agreements (covenants) with them. Noah and Abraham are two examples. God then makes an agreement with a whole nation (Israel), with the goal of spreading that relationship to the rest of the world. Christians believe that this plan was fulfilled in Jesus, who opened friendship with God to all people.

Useful websites

- http://commons.wikimedia.org (search by Adam and Eve, fall of Adam and Eve and garden of Eden/paradise)
- www.textweek.com/art/garden_of_eden.htm (use the scripture index for other information)
- www.biblical-art.com/biblicalsubject2.asp?id_biblicalsubject=22 (a huge number of images)

Script 1

Unpacking the bag

My bag is green/has leaves, like a garden in spring.
There is fruit in my bag, good to eat.
There are flowers in my bag, bright and beautiful.
There are animals in my bag; they are not frightened.
There are people in my bag who live in the garden.
There is a tree in my bag, and fruit that no one should eat.

The story

When the world was young, the Maker *(sign 'God')* made a garden *(place the cloth and smooth it)*. He filled it with flowers *(add flowers)* and plants that gave wonderful fruit *(add fruit)*. Animals lived there without fear, for no one hurt them *(add animals)*. The Maker *(sign 'God')* placed people in the garden and told them to enjoy it and care for it *(add people)*. So the people lived there in peace.

In the centre of the garden stood a tree *(add tree)*. The Maker *(sign 'God')* told the people never to eat the fruit of that tree *(add fruit)*, for that would ruin everything. One day a lying voice *(sign 'lie')* whispered to the people that they could eat the fruit from the tree that the Maker *(sign 'God')* had said no one should eat. The people listened *(cup ear)* to the lying voice and ate *(remove forbidden fruit)*, and their world changed.

The Maker *(sign 'God')* was sad *(sign 'sad')*. Wrong had crept into his world, and it began with a lie *(sign 'lie')* and a wrong choice *(sign 'choice')*. It was the beginning of the wrong that spoils our world. For us, there may be no tree *(lift tree)* and no fruit *(lift fruit)*, but there may be lying voices *(sign 'lie')*, and we have to decide whether we listen to them *(cup ear)* or not.

You will need
* A green bag, or one with a leaf pattern
* Screwed-up tissue paper in various colours for flowers
* Animals from an animal set
* Two people figures
* Screwed-up green tissue paper for a tree
* Rolled coloured tissue for fruits (or use pictures)
* A larger tissue paper fruit for the forbidden fruit

Questions
(See also page 11.)
* Why do you think the animals were not afraid?
* The people were given just one rule and they broke it. I wonder why.
* How can wrong spoil a world?
* Who was the Maker?

Reproduced with permission from *More Bible Storybags®* published by BRF 2012 (978 1 84101 836 2) www.barnabasinschools.org.uk

THE TESTING TREE (ADAM AND EVE MAKE A CHOICE)

You will need

* A green bag, or one with a leaf pattern
* Screwed-up tissue paper in various colours for flowers
* Animals from an animal set
* Two people figures
* A gift tag
* Screwed-up green tissue paper for a tree
* Rolled coloured tissue paper for fruits (or use pictures)
* A larger tissue paper fruit for the forbidden fruit

Script 2

Unpacking the bag

My bag is green/has leaves, like a garden in spring.
There is fruit in my bag, good to eat.
There are flowers in my bag, bright and beautiful.
There are animals in my bag, unafraid.
There are people in my bag who receive a gift.
There is a tree in my bag—a testing tree with fruit that no one should eat.

The story

Our story takes place on a green cloth…	*Place cloth*
for the Maker placed people in a garden.	*Add people*
In the garden, flowers bloomed…	*Add flowers*
trees hung heavy with fruit…	*Add fruit*
and animals slept secure.	*Add animals*
People trod the earth gently…	*Move people*
for this was the Maker's world, gifted to them…	*Add gift tag*
theirs to enjoy, theirs to rule, theirs to care.	
At the centre of the garden stood a tree…	*Add tree*
a testing tree whose fruit no one must eat.	*Add 'fruit' to tree*
That was the test.	
Peace circled the tree…	*Circle tree with finger*

Reproduced with permission from *More Bible Storybags*® published by BRF 2012 (978 1 84101 836 2) **www.barnabasinschools.org.uk**

THE TESTING TREE (ADAM AND EVE MAKE A CHOICE)

and radiated through the garden like the spokes of a wheel.	*Indicate with hands*
A lying voice whispered in the garden…	*Sign 'lie'*
calling the people to eat the fruit from the tree.	*Point to tree*
They listened to the voice…	*Cup ear*
and failed the test.	
The circle broke…	*Clap hands and let them fall*
the wheel cracked and the peace of the garden was shattered.	
Life changed in the garden: flowers still bloomed…	*Lift and replace flowers*
trees still hung heavy with fruit…	*Lift and replace fruit*
but animals no longer rested secure…	*Lift and replace animals*
and people no longer trod gently on the earth.	*Move people*
Life became a struggle: person against person…	*Make fists, bring knuckles together*
nation against nation…	*Make fists, bring knuckles together*
people against the animals…	*Make fists, bring knuckles together*
people against the land.	*Make fists, bring knuckles together*
For us, there may be no special trees…	*Lift and replace tree*
no forbidden fruit…	
but there will be lying voices…	*Sign 'lie'*
and listening is a choice.	*Sign 'choice'*

Questions
(See also page 11.)
* Who was the Maker? Whose was the lying voice?
* Why do you think there was a test in the garden?
* Do you think the test was fair?
* In what ways is the garden like our world?

Reproduced with permission from *More Bible Storybags®* published by BRF 2012 (978 1 84101 836 2) www.barnabasinschools.org.uk

THE TESTING TREE (ADAM AND EVE MAKE A CHOICE)

The tide

The story of Noah

Using the storybag® in assembly

> ✂ **You will need**
> * Coloured paper (see prayer)

> See the pastoral note on page 33.

Introduce the assembly by asking pupils what they know about rainbows, showing images if you have them (see, for example, http://commons.wikimedia.org/wiki/Rainbow). Explain that Christians have a story about the rainbow.

Today's story is about a promise and a new start. Read the Bible story. (An online turn-the-page book of Noah can be found on the website: www.refuel.org.uk/projects/ks1_topics/old testament/old_testament.html.)

> **Comment**
> An important theme from the story of Noah is new beginnings and being given a second chance. It is also the story of a promise that never again would the earth be flooded in this way. Noah and his family were given a chance to create a better world. Unfortunately, they made many of the same mistakes as the people before them, but God did not give up on them. God had a plan—but that is a story for another day.

Reflection

Use the storybag® script 1 or 2 as a reflection. It can be read by the teacher, with pupils adding gestures, sign language and sound. Pupils can also hold up objects and people from the bag. PowerPoint visuals of the story cloths can be accessed via www.barnabasinschools.org.uk/cooling2.

Prayer *(optional)*

Ask pupils to think about having a fresh start in life. Write the following prayer on different coloured pieces of paper that pupils can hold up and read.

Red: God of beginnings and second chances,
Orange: you gave a promise
Yellow: and put your bow in the sky.
Green: You gave people a new beginning,
Blue: a second chance.
Indigo: You put the bow in the heavens,
Violet: so that we could live our lives in the light of your promise.

NB: The song 'Sing a rainbow' can be used, but the first two lines need changing to fit the colours of the rainbow: 'Red and orange and yellow and green, indigo, violet and blue…'

Using the storybag® in RE

Introduce the subject using some of the material from the assembly introduction on page 32. On the same page you will find a comment on the biblical story. Select the appropriate script and turn to pages 9 and 10 to find ways of using it.

Biblical material

Genesis 6:9—9:17

Long ago, God looked down on the world and was sad, very sad, when he saw that people had become cruel and filled the world with violence. People spent their time thinking up new ways of hurting each other. God saw that his world was ruined, and it broke his heart, so he decided to start again.

God looked around and saw one family—Noah's family. They were different. Noah was a good man. God told Noah his plan and Noah obeyed and built a special boat called an ark. Into the ark he placed two of every creature and, finally, his own family.

The rains came and the waters rose and covered the earth. For 40 days it rained and the flood water rose, but the ark sailed on for many days more. Eventually, a great wind blew and began to dry the water. Noah sent a dove to see if there was any dry land. The dove returned with an olive leaf, a sign that the water had gone down a little and the trees could be seen. Noah waited a week and sent another dove out, but it never returned. It had found a home, so there must be dry land!

Noah and his family and all the animals left the ark and celebrated by worshipping God. They began a new life with God's blessing. They were given a fresh start, a second chance. 'As long as the earth remains, there will always be planting and harvest, cold and heat; winter and summer, day and night,' promised God. Then he painted a rainbow in the sky and said, 'The rainbow that I have put in the sky will be my sign to you… Never again will I let floodwaters destroy all life.'

'The rainbow will be a sign of that solemn promise,' said God.

Follow-up activities

Select from the following activities, according to the age and aptitude of your pupils. (See also pages 11 and 12.)

1. Create a wall display of this story that reflects the layout of the bag. Add two-dimensional versions of items from the story, such as paper people and pictures of animals. Sections of the script can act as captions. Add pupils' questions and comments and use them as a basis for discussion. Place the appropriate story script and an open children's Bible on a table. Add pupils' rainbows to the table.

2. Interpret elements of the story in dance, using fabric as an extension of pupils' bodies: wind, rain, waves, dove and rainbow. How could hope, celebration (worship) and a new beginning be expressed? Why do you think the first thing Noah did on reaching dry land was to worship God?

3. Create a rainbow cross in an El Salvador style (see, for example, www.gifts-of-faith.com/elsalvador/cross-rainbow.html). Divide a cross into five sections. In the centre, place the rainbow. Use the other sections to tell the story in pictures. Text can be added on the back of the cross, with an explanation of why the rainbow is in the centre.

4. The group can create rainbows in different media. Add the promises in the coloured bands. Why do you think this part of the story is important for Christians?

5. With older pupils, explore small sections of Benjamin Britten's children's opera *Noye's Fludde* (performances available to view online).
   Pupils can create a soundscape for the story. They can perform the sailor's hymn 'Eternal Father, strong to save' from *Noye's Fludde* (available online). What can they learn about how Christians feel about God from this hymn? How does this relate to the story of Noah?

6. Pupils can write a poem starting and ending with the name 'Noah', and using parts of the word ('No' or 'ah!' within the poem. For example:

Noah.
No good left in the land,
No notice taken of God.
No end to this rain…

Symbols used in the story

- Dove: the olive leaf and the dove have both come to symbolise peace.
- The rainbow: a symbol of promise and hope.
- Tears: God is described in the text as having a broken heart, and the tears represent this.

Signs used in the story (British Sign Language)

- Prayer as a conversation with God: palms together in prayer, then open them like a book and move palms up and down.
- 'God': point index finger of right hand upwards at shoulder height. Other digits curled inwards.

Useful websites

- www.christiansigns.org.uk (search 'vocab' for the words 'prayer' and 'God')
- www.signstation.org (go to the BSL dictionary, then A–Z)
- www.britishsignlanguage.com

Reflective activity

Create a rainbow reflection area or corner by putting rainbow-coloured fabric over a chair and adding blue paper for sky, with the promise written on it. Add a basket of rainbow stickers. Pupils can add a rainbow to

the sky and think about heat or cold, the seasons, day or night, planting and harvest, and what our world would be like without them.

Assessment

Assess the pupils' understanding by observing them replaying the script, or ask them to talk about the display or write about it.

Background information and understanding the story

- Christians differ over how they understand this story. Some understand it literally, while others see it as a story full of spiritual truth that possibly has its roots in a historical flood.
- Many nations, particularly in the Middle East, have a flood story that may indicate a devastating flood in that area. The biblical story differs from other flood stories in its meaning.
- God makes an agreement (covenant) with Noah, and the rainbow is a sign of that agreement.
- There are still floods, but the rainbow is God's promise that there will never be another flood of this type or scale. God also promises stability: there will always be cold and heat, day and night, and changing seasons.
- The story of Noah is almost creation in reverse, as the world reverts to a watery chaos.

Useful websites

- www.textweek.com/art/noah.htm (select scripture index for other information)
- www.refuel.org.uk/projects/ks1_topics/old_testament/old_testament.html (turn-the-page book)
- www.biblical-art.com/biblicalsubject2.asp?id_biblicalsubject=22 (lots of images)
- www.hcqigallery.com/shop/poster/new_posters.html (poster to purchase of Noah and his wife in the style of the film *Titanic*)
- http://christianity.about.com/od/symbolspictures/ig/Christian-Symbols-Glossary/Christian-Dove.htm
- http://christianity.about.com/od/symbolspictures/ig/Christian-Symbols-Glossary/Christian-Rainbow.htm

Script 1

Unpacking the bag

Our bag is the colour of sea water.
There are drops in my bag for rain and tears,
and a leaf that brings hope.
There are animals in my bag, two by two.
There is a boat in my bag and people who build it.
There is a dove and a rainbow in my bag, and both promise peace.
There are mugs, and spoons to tap them with. I wonder what they are for.

The story

Long ago, when the world was still young, people were cruel and all they thought about was doing wrong *(place cloth and smooth)*. Slowly, their wrong spread across the world like water *(undulate hand over cloth)*, until all was spoiled. The Maker *(sign 'God')* saw how cruel the people had become and his tears fell to the earth *(sprinkle tears)*, for he was sad that his beautiful world was ruined. Then the Maker *(sign 'God')* saw a man and his family *(place people figures)*. They were not cruel; they were good, and the Maker *(sign 'God')* smiled *(draw smile in the air)*.

The Maker *(sign 'God')* told the man to build a boat *(add boat)*, and that's what he did. The Maker *(sign 'God')* told the man to gather into the boat all the animals, two by two *(add animals to boat)*, and that's what he did. The Maker *(sign 'God')* told the man to bring his family into the boat *(add people figures to boat)*, and that's what he did. Then the rain began to fall *(drop raindrops, tap mug with spoon)* and the waters rose *(bunch cloth or raise hands)*.

For 40 days it rained and the boat sailed on the rising seas *(keep bunching and moving the cloth)*. Then the rain stopped and all was quiet *(finger on lips)*. Still the boat sailed on. The man sent a dove to see if there was any dry land *(sit dove on the palm of your hand and move your hand around)*. The dove came back with a leaf *(add leaf to dove and place both on the ark)*. The waters were going down *(flatten waves)*.

The Maker *(sign 'God')* told the man and his family to leave the boat and start a new world *(move people figures and animals out of the boat and off the bag)*, and that's what he did. Above shone a rainbow *(add rainbow to bag)*. It was the Maker's *(sign 'God')* sign that never again would such a flood cover the whole world. The Maker *(sign 'God')* promised that while the world existed, there would always be day and night, heat and cold, summer and winter, planting and harvest.

You will need
* A sea-coloured bag (grey-green or blue)
* Silver paper tears and raindrops
* Plastic mugs for making rain sounds, and spoons to tap them
* Four pairs of small animals (from children's animal set, or pictures)
* Eight people figures (Noah, wife, three sons and their wives)
* A boat (shoebox with boat shapes on the long sides)
* A paper dove and tissue paper leaf
* Rainbow cloth, tissue paper or rainbow stickers on a strip of paper (available from stationers)

Questions
(See also page 11.)
* What made the Maker sad? What made the Maker smile?
* Why do you think people became cruel?
* Why do you think the Maker gave a rainbow sign?

Reproduced with permission from *More Bible Storybags®* published by BRF 2012 (978 1 84101 836 2) www.barnabasinschools.org.uk

Older pupils

You will need

* A sea-coloured bag (grey-green or blue)
* Silver paper tears and raindrops
* Plastic mugs for making rain sounds, and spoons to tap them
* Four pairs of small animals (from a children's animal set, or pictures)
* Eight people figures (Noah, wife, three sons and their wives)
* A boat (shoebox with boat shapes on the long sides)
* Paper dove and tissue paper leaf
* Rainbow cloth, tissue paper or rainbow stickers on a strip of paper (available from stationers)
* Card saying 'The beginning...'

Script 2

● Unpacking the bag

Our bag is the colour of sea water.
There are drops in my bag for rain and tears.
There are animals in my bag, two by two.
There is a boat in my bag and people who build it.
There is a dove and a rainbow in my bag, and both promise peace.
There is a leaf in my bag, a sign of hope.
There are mugs, and spoons to tap them with. I wonder what they are for.
There is a card. What does it say?

● The story

Our story takes place on a sea-coloured cloth...	*Place cloth*
for this is the story of tides: tides of water, tides of wrong.	*Smooth cloth*
A long time ago, when the world was young, evil spread across the earth...	*Undulate hand over cloth*
like an incoming tide. In the heavens the Maker wept...	*Sign 'God'*
as he saw his creation...	*Sprinkle tears*
swept beneath a tide of violence.	
He would answer with a flood...	*Create waves in cloth*
to wash away the wrong...	*Smooth cloth*
and start again.	
But not all were evil.	*Shake head*
One man and his family were good.	*Place Noah*
He and his family would be the Maker's seed for a new world.	*Place family*

Reproduced with permission from *More Bible Storybags*® published by BRF 2012 (978 1 84101 836 2) www.barnabasinschools.org.uk

THE TIDE (THE STORY OF NOAH)

The man gathered his family and built a boat…	*Place boat*
that would float on the coming flood.	
It would sail across great waters…	*Undulate hand*
to bring them safe to land, to start again.	
They filled the boat with animals, great and glorious…	*Add animals*
small and sleek…	*Add animals*
wonderful and wild…	*Add animals*
tame and timid.	*Add animals*
The boat echoed with their noise.	*Hands over ears*
From above, the rain fell.	*Drop raindrops, tap mugs*
From below, the flood rose.	*Lift hands, gather cloth*
They drifted on the tide.	*Undulate hands*
They prayed as the waters rose…	*Sign 'prayer'*
then silence.	*Finger on lips*
The waters shrank, little by little.	*Smooth cloth a little*
The land emerged, little by little.	*Smooth cloth a little*
A dove brought a sign of peace…	*Add dove with leaf*
and the boat washed ashore on a tide of mercy.	*Move boat to edge*
High above, the Maker painted the sky with the colours of promise…	*Add rainbow*
and the people and animals spilled out into a new world.	*Move people and animals out*
The beginning…	*Add sign*

Questions
(See also page 11.)

* What is a tide? Can wrong be like a tide?
* Why does the Maker cry in this story?
* How would the people need to live, to stop the world going wrong again?
* What do you think the promise was?

Reproduced with permission from *More Bible Storybags®* published by BRF 2012 (978 1 84101 836 2) www.barnabasinschools.org.uk

THE TIDE (THE STORY OF NOAH)

The land of promises

Abraham and Sarah

Using the storybag® in assembly

 You will need

* Two pieces of A3 paper, rolled into scrolls. Inside one, write 'You will have children.' Inside the other, write 'You will have a land of your own.'

Introduce the story by setting up a promise relay around the room. Take the 'land' scroll and read it. Reroll it and have it passed from hand to hand around the room until it gets back to you. Imagine a special promise being passed in a different way down the generations: from mum and dad to their children and then to their children.

Using the 'children' scroll, set up the relay again, with the boys only: grandad to dad, to grandson, to great-grandson, to great-great-grandson, and so on. Repeat with the girls. It is like a message from the past.

Today's story is about promises that people waited a long time for. Read the Bible story on page 39.

Comment

This is a story about promises. One promise said that a couple called Abraham and Sarah would have children. This promise came true after a long wait. Their baby, Isaac, had children and so it continued.

The other promise, about having a land of their own, did not come true in Abraham and Sarah's lifetime. They passed the promise on to their son, Isaac, who passed it on to his son, Jacob, who passed it on to his son, Joseph, who passed it on to his son, Ephraim, who passed it on to his son, and so on for hundreds of years until one day, many years later, Abraham and Sarah's great-great-many times over-grandchildren had a land of their own. The promise finally came true.

Reflection

Use the storybag® script 1 or 2 as a reflection. It can be read by the teacher, with pupils performing any gestures, sign language or sounds. Pupils can also hold up objects and people from the bag. PowerPoint visuals of the story cloths can be accessed via www.barnabasinschools.org.uk/cooling2..

 Prayer (optional)

Lord, you called Abraham and he followed. You gave promises and he believed them. Help us to trust you like Abraham did, and to keep our promises.

Using the storybag® in RE

Introduce the subject using some of the material from the assembly introduction (see page 38). On the same page you will find a comment on the biblical story. Select the appropriate script and turn to pages 9 and 10 to find ways of using it.

Biblical material

Genesis 11:31–32; 12:1–9; 15:1–7; 17:1–8; 21:1–7; 22:17

Abraham and his wife Sarah lived in a town called Ur, but they moved with all their family—grannies and grandads, uncles and aunts, brothers and cousins—to a town called Haran. After a while, God called Abraham to leave Haran and his large family and go to a different country, far, far away. God promised that from Abraham's children he would make a great nation who would be a blessing to others. Abraham and Sarah had no children at the time, but they trusted God. They took a few members of their family with them and started the journey to Canaan.

When they arrived in Canaan, God gave Abraham two promises. The first promise was that they would have a child of their own. That child would have children, and those children would have children, until the family became so large that trying to count them would be like counting the stars in the sky or the grains of sand on the beach. The second promise was that one day they would have a land of their own.

Abraham and Sarah wandered around Canaan for many years and, when they were elderly, they had a baby boy called Isaac, which means 'laughter'. One promise had come true. Isaac grew up, and still the other promise had not come true, but Abraham and Sarah carried on believing. They trusted that one day their children's children would have a land of their own.

Follow-up activities

Select from the activities below, according to the age and aptitude of your pupils. (See also pages 11 and 12).

1. Create a display of this story that reflects the layout of the bag. Add two-dimensional versions of items from the story. Place the appropriate story script and an open children's Bible on a table. Add pupils' questions and comments, and use them as a basis for discussion. Add the promise scrolls and children's poems.

2. Give pupils some starter sentences to complete as Sarah and Abraham might have completed them: 'We left home because…'; 'We called our son "laughter" because…'; 'We believed the promises because…' and so on.

3. Abraham was told that his descendants would be as numerous as the stars in the sky (Genesis 22:17). What does this simile communicate? Create other similes to communicate huge numbers—for example, 'as many as the snowflakes in a blizzard' and so on. They can be put together as a class simile poem. Add introductory and closing lines to the poem.

4. Practise passing a baton from one person to another. Discuss the passing on of a promise from one generation to another. What would be hard about waiting so long? What might help someone to believe the promise? What do pupils find it hard to wait for? What helps them wait? Add pupils' comments to the display.

5. Abraham was told that his people would be a blessing to others. In what ways can a person be a blessing to others? How could we be a blessing to others?

6. Write the story of Abraham on a long strip of paper to create a 'pathway story'. Apply star stickers at important moments and words, and discuss why they are important.

Symbols used in the story

☉ Stars and sand: symbols of things too numerous to count.

Signs used in the story (British Sign Language)

☉ 'No': hand waved back and forth across face.
☉ 'God': right hand at shoulder level, right index finger points upward, other digits curled inwards.

Useful websites

☉ www.signstation.org (go to the BSL dictionary, then A–Z for the word 'no')
☉ www.christiansigns.org.uk (search 'vocab' for the word 'God')
☉ www.britishsignlanguage.com

Reflective activity

Give pupils a star to add to the display, and ask them to think of promises that have been important to them.

Assessment

Assess the pupils' understanding by observing them replaying the script, or ask them to talk about the display or write about it.

Background information and understanding the story

- ✪ Abraham was born in Ur, in what is now Southern Iraq, and then moved to Haran in the north (modern south-east Turkey). The move to Canaan (modern Israel) as a semi-nomad would have been a big change, as Ur was a highly developed culture. (Visit www.britishmuseum.org and search for 'Ur'.)
- ✪ Abraham's journey was probably part of a movement of Semitic peoples that took place around 2000bc. The names of the people in the biblical story are reflected in finds from the Ur and Haran areas at this period.
- ✪ Abraham felt that God was calling him to leave his home town (where people worshipped many gods) and go to Canaan. Abraham worshipped only one God, called 'El', which means 'God'.
- ✪ This was unusual in an age when many gods were worshipped. Subsequently, this God introduces himself as the God of Abraham, Isaac and Jacob.
- ✪ In the Bible, God's call comes in many ways—through an actual 'voice', through a vision. or through special dreams and circumstances. For Christians, God's 'call' to a particular place or vocation might come through thoughts, events, Bible reading or a person's own God-given gifts and interests. It would be discussed with others and prayed over.

Useful websites

- ✪ www.textweek.com/art/abraham.htm (select scripture index for other information)
- ✪ http://commons.wikimedia.org (search by Abraham)
- ✪ www.biblical-art.com/biblicalsubject2.asp?id_ biblicalsubject=23

Script 1

Unpacking the bag

My bag is plain but with many paths, for this is a story of a journey.
There are people in my bag—a man and his wife
and a baby who grows up.
There are promises in the bag—one, two.
There are footprints in the bag that are left across the land.
There are stars in the bag, too many to count.

The story

Our story takes place on a cloth with many paths, for this is a story of a journey *(place bag, trace lines with your finger)*. In a distant land, a man and his wife *(place Abraham and Sarah)* live with their family: aunts and uncles, grannies and grandads. The couple pack their bags and leave their home *(move Abraham and Sarah)*. They are going on a journey to another land.

God is calling them to follow him *(move people along a path)*. The man and his wife follow and are given two promises *(show promise scrolls, read them, scatter stars, place scrolls on the bag)*. They wander the land for many years *(move people)*, leaving their footprints *(place footprints)*.

When they are elderly and hope is almost gone, a child is born *(place baby)*. They call him 'laughter', for he brings much joy. The child grows *(replace with adult Isaac)* and they grow older but still they have no land of their own *(sign 'no')*. Will this promise come true? One day, will their child or his children leave footprints in a land of their own? *(Add more footprints.)*

You will need
* A white bag with wiggly lines on it
* Three people figures and a baby (Abraham, Sarah, adult Isaac, baby Isaac)
* Two paper scrolls with the following written on them: (Scroll 1) 'You will have children and your children's children will be so many they will be like the stars in the sky' and (Scroll 2) 'One day you will have a land of your own.'
* Small paper footprints (available as stickers from stationers or craft shops)
* A packet of small paper stars (available as stickers from stationers or craft shops)

Questions
(See also page 11.)
* Why do you think the man and his wife left home?
* Why do you think they gave their son a name that means 'laughter'?
* Do you think the other promise will come true?

Reproduced with permission from *More Bible Storybags*® published by BRF 2012 (978 1 84101 836 2) www.barnabasinschools.org.uk

THE LAND OF PROMISES (ABRAHAM AND SARAH)

You will need

* A white bag with wiggly lines on it
* Three people figures and a baby (man, woman, adult Isaac, baby Isaac)
* Two small paper scrolls, one with 'Children' written on it, and the other with 'Land' written on it
* Small paper footprints (available as stickers from craft shops or stationers)
* Two pieces of paper showing the words 'Leave your people'
* Two pieces of paper showing the words 'Leave your land'
* Two pieces of paper showing the words 'Leave your gods'
* Two pieces of paper showing the word 'Follow'

Script 2

Unpacking the bag

My bag is plain but with many paths, for this is a story of journeys.
There are people in the bag—a man and his wife
and a baby who grows up.
There are promises in the bag—one, two.
There are footprints in the bag that are left across the land.
There are words in our bag, important for our story.

The story

Our story takes place…	*Place bag*
on a cloth with many paths…	*Trace paths with finger*
for this is a story of many journeys.	
It is the story of a man and his wife…	*Place two people*
who followed.	
Words sang in the wind…	*Soft wind noise*
calling, calling.	
The man had heard it all his life…	*Soft wind noise*
the voice on the wind.	
It called him to leave his people…	*Blow away 'Leave your people' (1) from your hand*
leave his land…	*Blow away 'Leave your land' (1)*
leave his gods…	*Blow away 'Leave your gods' (1)*
and follow.	*Blow away 'Follow' (1)*
The man and his wife followed.	*Move people*
They left behind their people…	*Blow away 'Leave your people' (2)*
their lands…	*Blow away 'Leave your land' (2)*
their gods…	*Blow away 'Leave your gods' (2)*

Reproduced with permission from *More Bible Storybags*® published by BRF 2012 (978 1 84101 836 2) www.barnabasinschools.org.uk

THE LAND OF PROMISES (ABRAHAM AND SARAH)

and followed.	*Blow away 'Follow' (2)*
Across deserts and plains…	*Move people along a path*
over hills and valleys…	*Bunch cloth*
they followed the voice…	*Move people along a path*
to a land of promises.	
Promise of land.	*Show scroll and place*
Promise of children.	*Show scroll and place*
Promise that the one who called would be their God, and it was so.	*Sign 'God'*
But they were without a child…	*Lift 'Children' scroll and replace*
and without land.	*Lift 'Land' scroll and replace*
Still the man and his wife followed…	*Move people along paths*
chasing promises in hope.	
When hope had almost gone, a promise came true: a child was born…	*Add baby and remove 'Children' scroll*
who brought joy and laughter.	
The child grew into a man…	*Add adult Isaac and remove baby*
and still they hoped for land.	
In old age, the man passed the promise of land to his son to keep it safe.	*Move scroll to Isaac*
He left behind his footprints on the land…	*Add footprints*
that was not yet his.	
But someday his children's children would place their footprints…	*Add footprints*
on a land that would be theirs.	

Questions
(See also page 11.)
* Whose was the voice that called on the wind?
* Why do you think the man and his wife followed?
* Why do you think they had to wait so long for the promises to come true?

Reproduced with permission from *More Bible Storybags*® published by BRF 2012 (978 1 84101 836 2) www.barnabasinschools.org.uk

THE LAND OF PROMISES (ABRAHAM AND SARAH)

The coloured coat

Joseph is sold as a slave

> ✂ **You will need**
> * A4 cards, some with 'True' written on them, some with 'False'

Introduce the story by playing a game. Three teachers recount an appropriate incident and pupils have to guess which one is telling the truth. Give a panel of pupils some cards to hold up with 'True' or 'False' on them. Other pupils can also vote. Explain that it is only a game.

There are different ways of not telling the truth: we may fail to tell the truth by what we say or what we do. Today's story is about great sadness that was caused by a cruel action and not telling the truth. Listen to the story and see if you can spot the people who are not telling the truth, by their actions or by silence.

Read the Bible story on page 45 or from the website www.topmarks.co.uk/judaism/joseph/joseph.htm.

Comment

The brothers dipped Joseph's coat in blood to make their father think he had been eaten by a wild animal. But this wasn't true: instead they had sold him as a slave. The brothers allowed their father to believe something that was untrue by what they did and by silence, not by what they said. Truthfulness is not only about telling the truth; it is about being honest in what we do. Selling Joseph as a slave was bad enough, but they added to the cruelty by leaving their father sad and grieving for Joseph's death when, in reality, Joseph was alive.

Reflection

Use the storybag® script 1 or 2 as a reflection. It can be read by the teacher, with pupils performing any gestures, sign language or sounds. Pupils can also hold up objects and people figures from the bag. PowerPoint visuals of the story cloths can be accessed via www.barnabasinschools.org.uk/cooling2.

Prayer *(optional)*

The BSL sign for 'truth' is the edge of the right palm striking the centre of the left palm (see www.britishsignlanguage.com/words/index.php?id=83). You may wish to use this sign in the prayer below.

God of truth, whose very nature is truth, help us to reflect your truthful nature in the way we live, by what we say and what we do.

Introduce the subject using some of the material from the assembly introduction (see page 44). On the same page you will find a comment on the biblical story. Select the appropriate script and turn to pages 9 and 10 to find ways of using it.

Biblical material

Genesis 37; 39:1—40:23

Jacob had twelve sons: ten older boys, a teenager called Joseph and little Benjamin. Joseph was his father's favourite and Jacob spoiled him. He gave Joseph a coat of many colours to show that Joseph was his favourite son. The older boys hated Joseph and their hatred was made worse by Joseph telling tales about the brothers and telling them his dreams.

'I dreamed that we were cutting the wheat and your sheaves of wheat bowed down to mine. Then I had another dream. There were eleven stars and the sun and moon, and they all bowed down to me,' he said.

Everyone was upset, even Jacob. How dare the boy think he was so important that people would bow down to him?

One day, Joseph visited his older brothers while they were looking after the sheep. 'Here comes the dreamer,' they chorused. 'Let's kill him and be rid of him.'

'No!' said Reuben. 'Just put him in a hole in the ground for a while.' (He planned to rescue Joseph later.)

While Reuben was checking the sheep, the others saw some traders passing by. 'Let's sell him,' they said; 'at least we'll get some money for him.' So Joseph was sold for 20 pieces of silver and taken away to be sold on as a slave.

Reuben came back to find Joseph missing, and the others told him what they had done. Reuben was horrified. He knew his father would be heartbroken. Together the boys came up with a plan. They dipped Joseph's coat in animal blood and took it to their father.

'We found this coat. Is it Joseph's?'

'Yes,' said Jacob, 'it is his. He must have been killed by a wild animal.'

None of the older brothers said a word.

Jacob cried and thought he would never smile again. He had lost his favourite son. Meanwhile, far away in Egypt, Joseph was sold as a slave to a rich man called Potiphar.

Joseph became a slave in Potiphar's house. He did well and was soon trusted to look after the whole house. Just when life was getting better, Mrs Potiphar told a lie and Joseph was sent to prison, even though he had done no wrong. In prison, Joseph was sad, but he soon became trusted by the guards and was put in charge of other prisoners. One prisoner was the king's chief cook, another was his personal servant and both had strange dreams. Joseph told them that their dreams meant that one would die and one would serve wine to the king, and that is what happened.

Joseph asked the king's personal servant to remember him, but the servant forgot all about him and Joseph stayed in prison.

Follow-up activities

Select from the activities below, according to the age and aptitude of your pupils. (See also pages 11 and 12.)

1. Create a two-dimensional display of this story that reflects the layout of the bag (see images on inside front cover). Add two-dimensional versions of items from the story. Place the appropriate story script and an open children's Bible on a table. Add questions and pupils' comments, and use them as a basis for discussion.

2. Use finger puppets or hand puppets to retell the story. Pupils can write lines for their puppet or a script for the story. Pupils can write or say their thoughts about the story.

3. Explore a song from the musical *Joseph and the Amazing Technicolor Dreamcoat*. Choose one that reflects this early part of the story. Evaluate the song, considering how well it reflects the biblical story and its meaning.

4. In drama, develop the line, 'If only…'. How would the following characters have completed this sentence—the older brothers, Joseph and Jacob? Discuss how we deal with regret through saying sorry and making amends, putting things right where we can and learning from the experience.

5. Tell the story of Joseph from different points of view—the father's and the older brothers'. What insights does this give into the story? What is your verdict on this part of the Joseph story? How would you assess the characters?

6. How did the lie affect each of the characters' lives? In what way was the lie like a poison? Write your responses on an outline of a bottle marked 'poison'.

Symbols used in the story

- ✪ Coloured coat: a symbol of favour.
- ✪ Poison: a symbol of lying and what it does in people's lives.

Signs used in the story (British Sign Language)

- ✪ 'Sad': right hand held vertically in front of the face, side on. Move downward to just below the chin.
- ✪ 'God': point index finger of right hand upwards at shoulder height, other digits curled inwards.

Useful websites

- ✪ www.christiansigns.org.uk (search 'vocab' for the word 'God')
- ✪ www.britishsignlanguage.com (for the word 'sad')
- ✪ www.signstation.org (go to the BSL dictionary, then A–Z)

Reflective activity

Listen to 'Poor, poor Joseph' from the musical. Joseph did not just feel sorry for himself when things went wrong. What did he do? How do we react when things go badly? What can we learn from Joseph's story?

Assessment

Assess the pupils' understanding by observing them replaying the script, or ask them to talk about the display or write about it.

Background information and understanding the story

- ✪ Some scholars think that Joseph may have entered Egypt under the Hyksos Pharaohs, who were of Semitic origins, like Joseph. Scholars are divided about this.
- ✪ Coloured dyes were expensive, especially colours such as red and purple. A multicoloured coat was a very expensive item.

✪ The dreams mentioned in the story would have been seen as very special. Joseph insisted that he could only understand them with God's help. Reassure children about their own dreams.

Useful websites

- ✪ www.josephthemusical.com
- ✪ www.bbc.co.uk/religion/religions/judaism/history/joseph.shtml
- ✪ www.textweek.com/art/joseph_OT.htm (use the scripture index for other information)
- ✪ www.topmarks.co.uk/judaism/joseph/joseph.htm
- ✪ www.biblical-art.com/biblicalsubject2.asp?id_biblicalsubject=23 (a huge number of images)

Script 1

Unpacking the bag

My bag is purple: I wonder why.
There is a family in my bag: a boy, ten older brothers and one little
brother. We will meet lots of other people.
There are tears in the bag, coins and special dreams.
There is a coat of many colours and other coats to wear.

The story

Our story takes place on a purple bag, the colour of sorrow *(place bag)*,
but this story does not start with sadness. This is the story of a boy called
J who wore a coloured coat *(place boy, add coloured coat)*. J had ten big
brothers *(count to ten, place older brother figures)* and one little brother
called Ben *(wiggle little finger, add Benjamin)*. The ten big brothers
(count as before) hated J; he was proud, he was spoilt and he always got
the best. He dreamed *(add dream cloud)* that one day they would bow to
him and he would rule them all.

'No way!' said the ten brothers *(count as before)*.

The brothers could stand it no more. They took away J's coloured coat
(remove coat) and sold him to some men *(add coins)* who took him far,
far away *(move Joseph off the cloth)*. The brothers put animal blood on J's
coat *(turn coat red side out)* and took it to their dad, who cried for J, for
he thought the boy was dead *(add tears, remove all figures and items
with a sweep of the arm so that the bag is empty)*. Life seemed sorrowful
and sad *(sign 'sad' together)*, but God *(sign 'God')* was watching *(point to
eye)* and God *(sign 'God')* had a plan.

Far, far away *(point to the distance)* in a distant land, J still lived *(add
Joseph)*, but lonely now without his family. But he was not alone *(shake
head)*; God was there *(sign 'God')*. J was sold as a slave in a rich man's
house *(add figure with yellow tunic, add money)*. J grew into a man
(stretch or change figure). He worked hard and did well as a slave. Before
long he was in charge of the whole house *(indicate whole of bag)*, but the
lady of the house *(add figure with pink tunic)* told a lie and J was sent to
prison *(sweep off everything with your arm)*. Life seemed sorrowful and
sad *(sign 'sad' together)*, but God *(sign 'God')* was watching *(point to eye)*
and God *(sign 'God')* had a plan.

In the prison cell, J felt hurt and upset, for he had done no wrong
(place Joseph on his own). J was liked by the guards *(place two guards in
brown)* and they trusted him, so they gave him other prisoners to care for
(add two prisoners in grey). Two prisoners had two special dreams *(add
dream clouds)* and J told them what their dreams meant. 'Your dreams
mean that one of you will die and one will serve wine to the king,' he said.

You will need
* A purple bag
* Twelve people figures
  (ten older brothers,
  Joseph, Benjamin)
* Coloured coat: folded
  oblong of red felt
  with hole for head;
  add thin coloured
  ribbons
* Felt oblongs with
  central holes for the
  head to use as tunics:
  two brown, two grey,
  one yellow, one pink.
  These are needed
  to distinguish the
  people, as the same
  figures take different
  parts
* Coins
* Silver paper tears
* Two white dream
  clouds made from
  either white paper
  or felt

THE COLOURED COAT (JOSEPH IS SOLD AS A SLAVE)

And that is what happened *(remove one prisoner)*. 'Don't forget me,' said J to the servant. 'Remember how I helped you when you were in prison' *(remove other prisoner)*. But the king's servant forgot all about J *(sweep off everything with your arm)*. Life behind bars seemed sorrowful and sad *(sign 'sad' together)*, but God *(sign 'God')* was watching *(point to eye)* and God *(sign 'God')* had a plan.

Questions

(See also page 11.)

* Why do you think the father spoiled one boy?
* Why did the brothers not tell the father that the boy was alive?
* What do you think God's plan was?

Reproduced with permission from *More Bible Storybags*® published by BRF 2012 (978 1 84101 836 2) www.barnabasinschools.org.uk

THE COLOURED COAT (JOSEPH IS SOLD AS A SLAVE)

Script 2

Unpacking the bag

My bag is purple: I wonder why.
There is a family in my bag: a boy, ten older brothers and one little
brother. We will meet lots of other people.
There are tears in the bag, coins and special dreams with meanings.
There is a coat of many colours, red on the inside, and other coats to wear.
There are coins in my bag, and a bottle marked 'Poison'.

The story

You will need
* A purple bag
* Twelve people figures (ten older brothers, Joseph, Benjamin)
* Coloured coat: folded oblong of red felt with hole for head; add thin coloured ribbons
* Felt oblongs with central holes for the head to use as tunics: two brown, two grey, one yellow, one pink. These are needed to distinguish the people, as the same figures take different parts
* Coins
* Two dream clouds made from either white paper or felt
* Small plastic bottle marked 'poison'

Our story takes place on a purple cloth…	*Place cloth*
for this is a sad story—but it does not start that way.	
This is J. He wears a coloured coat.	*Place Joseph wearing coat*
These are his ten big brothers… 1, 2, 3, 4, 5, 6, 7, 8, 9, 10…	*Place older brothers one at a time as you count with pupils*
and one little brother called Ben	*Wiggle little finger and add Benjamin*
The big brothers hate J.	*Lift and replace Joseph*
He is spoilt; he is proud; he is their father's favourite.	
J dreams of power and fame, and tells his family so.	*Place two dream clouds*
The big brothers ten feel their anger rising…	
1, 2, 3, 4, 5, 6, 7, 8, 9, 10…	*Count with pupils (crossly)*
'What makes you so important?'	*Lift and bang down one brother*
'What makes you so proud?'	*Lift and bang down another brother*
'We will not bow to you!'	*Lift and bang down another brother*
The big brothers ten make a secret plan…	
1, 2, 3, 4, 5, 6, 7, 8, 9, 10.	*Count with pupils (whispering)*
They sell their brother to work as a slave…	*Remove Joseph and take off his coat*
swapping him for money they can use instead.	*Drop money on bag*
They take his coat and dip it in blood, sending the colours red.	*Place coat red side out*

Reproduced with permission from *More Bible Storybags*® published by BRF 2012 (978 1 84101 836 2) www.barnabasinschools.org.uk

THE COLOURED COAT (JOSEPH IS SOLD AS A SLAVE)

The big brothers ten know what they have done…	
1, 2, 3, 4, 5, 6, 7, 8, 9, 10.	*Count with pupils (sadly)*
They lie to their father about the boy, and the lie they told becomes part of their lives…	
a slow and deadly poison they cannot cure.	*Place poison bottle*
None of the brothers speak of the boy and the silence grows as the years go by.	*Finger on lips*
All seems lost…	*Sweep everything off the cloth with your arm*
but God is watching and God has a plan.	*Sign 'God', point to eye, sign 'God'*
Far, far away, J is sold.	*Add coins and Joseph*
He becomes a slave in a rich man's house…	*Add person in yellow tunic*
but a woman tells a lie…	*Add person in pink tunic*
and once again the poison works.	*Add poison bottle*
J finds himself behind prison bars. All seems lost…	*Sweep everything off the cloth with your arm*
but God is watching and God has a plan.	*Sign 'God', point to eye, sign 'God'*
Inside the jail, J sets to work.	*Place Joseph*
He wins the trust of the prison guards…	*Place two guards in brown tunics*
who place other prisoners in his care.	*Place two prisoners in grey tunics*
One night the prisoners have strange dreams…	*Place dream clouds*
and they ask J what their dreams mean.	
'One will leave to serve the king…	*Lift one prisoner*
and one will leave this jail to die.'	*Lift the other prisoner*
And that's what happened…	*Remove one prisoner*
just as J said. As the last prisoner leaves…	*Remove last prisoner*
J calls, 'Remember me.' But the man forgets. All seems lost…	*Sweep everything off the cloth with your arm*
but God is watching and God has a plan.	*Sign 'God', touch eye, sign 'God'*

Questions

(See also page 11.)

* Who do you think is at fault in this story?
* How can a lie be like poison?
* What do you think is God's plan?

Reproduced with permission from *More Bible Storybags*® published by BRF 2012 (978 1 84101 836 2) www.barnabasinschools.org.uk

THE COLOURED COAT (JOSEPH IS SOLD AS A SLAVE)

Together again

Joseph reconciled to his brothers

Using the storybag® in assembly

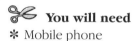
You will need
* Mobile phone

Introduce the story by talking about keeping in touch with friends and family. How do we do this? (Email, text, letters, cards, telephone and so on.) Two members of staff could phone or text each other.

Today's story is about a family that lost contact with one of its brothers, not because the family forgot or was lazy but because a great wrong had been done. Read the Bible story on page 52. (The previous part of the story can be found on page 45.) See also www.topmarks.co.uk/judaism/joseph/joseph.htm.

> **Comment**
> For many, many years, Joseph's family had no contact with him. His brothers had sold him as a slave and did not know what had happened to him. His father, Jacob, thought Joseph had been eaten by a wild animal, but he was alive and living far away in Egypt. The families in the Bible do not always get things right, but the family in this story learned that forgiveness can bring people together.

Reflection

Use the storybag® script 1 or 2 as a reflection. It can be read by the teacher, with pupils performing any gestures, sign language or sounds. Pupils can also hold up objects and people figures from the bag. PowerPoint visuals of the story cloths can be accessed via www.barnabasinschools.org.uk/cooling2.

Prayer (optional)

Forgiving God, help us to echo your forgiveness in our lives. Teach us to offer forgiveness with grace and to receive it with gratitude.

Using the storybag® in RE

Introduce the subject using some of the material from the assembly introduction (see page 51). On the same page you will find a comment on the biblical story. Select the appropriate script and turn to pages 9 and 10 to find ways of using it.

Biblical material

Genesis 41—45

For the first part of this story, see page 45.

Joseph was left in prison and the king's personal servant forgot all about him until, one day, the king (Pharaoh) had a strange dream. The king dreamed that seven fat cows and seven thin cows came from the river, and the seven thin cows ate the seven fat cows but did not get any fatter. The king was worried. What could this mean?

The king's personal servant remembered the man in prison who had told him what his dream meant. The king sent for Joseph, who explained that the seven fat cows meant seven years when crops that give food would grow. The seven thin cows were seven years when the crops would not grow and there would be hunger—unless something was done.

The king was impressed with Joseph and made him governor of Egypt. As Joseph said, after seven years the crops did not grow, but Joseph had stored crops in the good years, so no one went hungry.

Far away, Joseph's family was hungry and Joseph's ten older brothers came to buy food. Joseph recognised them as his long-lost brothers, but they did not recognise him and Joseph did not tell them who he was. Joseph decided to test them to see if they had changed. He accused them of being spies.

'No!' said the brothers. 'We are honest men, all from one family.' Privately they spoke among themselves, thinking Joseph could not understand them. 'This is happening because of what we did to Joseph all those years ago. We never listened to him when he pleaded with us not to sell him as a slave.'

Joseph pretended not to believe them, but he gave them food and sent them home. He told them that, to prove they were not spies, they must return with their little brother Benjamin. To make sure they came back, he kept one brother with him. Joseph had another test to show whether they were honest men: he put money in the sacks of food.

When the brothers got home, they found the money and were terrified. What if they were accused of stealing it? They had no idea how it had got there. They decided to keep it safe and return it. Their father was not happy about sending Benjamin to Egypt, but they needed more food so he let him go. The brothers promised to keep him safe.

The brothers went back to Egypt and tried to return the money. This proved that they were honest men, so Joseph said they could keep it. Joseph was overjoyed to see his little brother but still none of the brothers recognised him. Were they really changed men? Joseph decided on one last test. He gave them food and sent them home, but he hid a silver cup in Benjamin's sack.

Once they had set off for home, Joseph sent soldiers to look in the sacks. They found the cup in Benjamin's sack and Benjamin was arrested.

The brothers were upset, and one spoke up: 'Please don't keep our youngest brother. Our father will die of sadness if he does not come back. Take me instead. I will be your slave.'

That was all Joseph needed to hear. Now he knew they were changed men. He told the brothers who he was and told them not to worry about what they did in the past. God had brought good out of that wrong action and many lives had been saved. They could be together as a family again.

Follow-up activities

Select from the activities below, according to the age and aptitude of your pupils. (See also pages 11 and 12.)

1. Create a two-dimensional display of this story that reflects the layout of the bag. Add two-dimensional versions of items from the story. Place the appropriate story script and an open children's Bible on a table. Add questions and pupils' comments, and use them as a basis for discussion.

2. Create stepping stones of all or part of the Joseph story. Write the story events on pieces of paper cut out as stone shapes, and ask pupils to arrange them

in the correct order. Tape the stones on to the wall at pupil height. The line can wend its way around the hall or classroom wall. Ask pupils to walk the story and decide if the stones are in the right order and if any need adding. Different coloured stones can be added for pupils' comments, questions and links to experience. Photograph the stepping stones.

3. At the end of the story, Joseph says that good has come out of being sold as a slave in Egypt. What did he mean? Does this help us to understand the story? Imagine Joseph telling the story of his life to his children. What do you think he would remember as important?

4. Hold a discussion to explore the question 'Was Joseph right to test his brothers?' Prepare the discussion with arguments for and against. Think about the following questions. What was Joseph testing? Was the test appropriate? Did it show what he wanted it to show?

5. Create storylines for different characters (lines with events marked on them). Add thoughts and feelings for each character. Put the storylines for all the characters together on the display and write your comments on the story as a whole.

6. Create an 'art gallery' of paintings of Joseph (see websites listed below). Give pupils a range of comments to choose from for each painting, such as 'shows people's feelings'. Alternatively, pupils can write their own comments on sticky notes. Use the gallery and comments as a basis for discussion.

Symbols used in the story

☸ Fist: symbol of holding on to resentment.

Signs used in the story (British Sign Language)

☸ 'Sad': right hand held vertically in front of the face, side on. Move downward to just below the chin.
☸ 'Happy': right palm brushes left palm in a sliding clap.
☸ 'No': right hand waved back and forth across face.
☸ 'God': right hand at shoulder level, right index finger points upward, other digits curled inwards.

Useful websites

☸ www.signstation.org (go to the BSL dictionary, then A–Z for the words 'no' and 'happy')
☸ www.christiansigns.org.uk (search 'vocab' for the word 'God')
☸ www.britishsignlanguage.com (for the word 'sad')

Reflective activity

Ask pupils to close fists. Sometimes we hang on to resentment and bad feelings. Forgiveness means letting those feelings go. Ask pupils to open their hands. Explain that forgiveness does not mean letting people bully or hurt you.

Assessment

Assess the pupils' understanding by observing them replaying the script, or ask them to talk about the display or write about it.

Background information and understanding the story

(See also page 46.)

☸ Egyptian pictorial records show Asiatic people in brightly coloured robes coming to trade with Egypt. Joseph's brothers would probably have been classed as 'Asiatics' by the Egyptians, for this is what they called people from the region of Canaan. Images can be viewed online: search by 'Beni Hasan tomb paintings'.
☸ Jacob treated Joseph and Benjamin better than he treated his other sons because they were the sons of his favourite wife, Rachel. This led to bad feeling in the family. Few people are free of guilt in this story. Joseph is spoilt and proud; the brothers are scheming and cruel. Only Reuben, the eldest, emerges with integrity. Biblical families are often shown as flawed and sometimes dysfunctional, but God still cares for them and continues to work through them.
☸ Joseph says that God used the events for good, in order to save many lives. Joseph was the right person in the right place when famine came. That does not mean the brothers were right to sell Joseph as a slave; it means that good can be brought out of wrong. The good outcome does not justify the wrong.
☸ In the Bible, to remember is often to act. We tend to use the word 'remember' to mean just thoughts. Joseph decided not to dwell on his brothers' misdeeds and not to act in revenge.

Useful websites

☸ www.topmarks.co.uk/judaism/joseph/joseph.htm
☸ www.textweek.com/art/joseph_OT.htm (use the scripture index for other information)
☸ www.biblical-art.com/biblicalsubject2.asp?id_biblicalsubject=22 (a huge number of images)
☸ http://commons.wikimedia.org/wiki/Bread
☸ www.biblical-art.com/biblicalsubject2.asp?id_biblicalsubject=23

Script 1

Unpacking the bag

My bag is colourful, for this is a story that ends in joy.
There are brothers in my bag—one long-lost brother
and a king with a crown.
There is a heart, and a collar that important people wore.
There's a dreaming cloud and tears of joy and food for hungry people.

The story

In a land far away *(place bag)*, a king had a dream *(place king)*, a puzzling dream *(add cloud)* of seven *(count together)*, yes, seven fat *(widen hands)* cows and seven *(count together)*, yes, seven thin cows *(place hands close together)*. Who could tell him what the puzzling dream meant? It was then that the king's personal servant remembered J. J was brought from prison to the king *(add Joseph)*.

'For seven years,' said J *(count to seven together)*, 'the crops will grow and there will be food *(move hands upwards to indicate growth)*. After that, for seven years *(count seven together)*, the crops won't grow and there will be little food' *(move hands downwards to indicate lack of growth)*.

The king was pleased and made J governor of Egypt *(place collar round shoulders of Joseph figure)*. J became an important man in the land. He stored the food *(place pictures of bread one on top of the other)* in the seven good years *(count together)*. In the seven bad years *(count together)* there was enough saved for everyone to eat *(spread some of the bread; sweep off everything with your arm)*.

Life was changing. It was no longer sorrowful and sad *(shake head, sign 'sad' together)*, and God *(sign 'God')* was watching *(point to eye)*, for this was God's plan *(sign 'God')* to save many lives.

Far away, the brothers were hungry *(rub stomach, place brothers on edge of cloth)* and they came to the land where J lived to buy food *(add Joseph, move brothers close)*. They did not know J was the brother they had sold so long ago *(lift Joseph)*. J had changed so much! J cried to see his brothers *(drop tears)* after such a long time. He tested their hearts to see if they had changed *(place heart)*. Finding them changed, he decided to forgive. The family was together again *(place them all together)*.

Life had changed. It was no longer sorrowful and sad *(shake head, sign 'sad')* but joyful *(sign 'happy')*, for God *(sign 'God')* had been watching *(point to eye)* and God *(sign 'God')* had made a plan to save many lives.

Reproduced with permission from *More Bible Storybags®* published by BRF 2012 (978 1 84101 836 2) www.barnabasinschools.org.uk

TOGETHER AGAIN (JOSEPH RECONCILED TO HIS BROTHERS)

You will need

* A colourful bag
* 13 people figures in mixed colours, one with a paper crown
* Pictures of bread
* Silver paper tears
* A white dream cloud made either from paper or felt
* Collar of yellow or gold made from paper or felt for Joseph as governor of Egypt
* Paper or felt heart shape

Questions
(See also page 11.)

* How do you think J tested his brothers to see if they had changed?
* Why do you think J forgave his brothers?
* What was God's plan?

Script 2

Unpacking the bag

My bag is colourful, for this is a story that ends in joy.
There are brothers in my bag—one long-lost brother
and a king with a crown.
There is a collar in my bag and bread for hungry people.
There's a dreaming cloud in my bag.

The story

Our story takes place on a colourful cloth…	*Place cloth*
for this is a story of joy.	
The king went to bed…	*Lie king down*
and dreamed a strange dream…	*Add dream cloud*
of seven cows fat and seven cows thin.	
'What does this mean?' asked the puzzled king.	*Stand king up*
'Who can explain my troubling dream?'	
Then a servant remembered J, and J was brought from his prison cell.	*Add Joseph*
J stood quietly before the king and told him the meaning of his troubling dream.	
'For seven years the crops will grow…	*Count to seven on fingers*
then for seven years the crops will fail.	*Count to seven on fingers*
Act now and your people will have food.'	
The king made J governor of Egypt.	*Add collar*

You will need
* A colourful bag
* 13 people figures in mixed colours, one with a paper crown
* Pictures of bread
* White dream cloud made from either paper or felt
* Collar made from yellow or gold paper or felt

Reproduced with permission from *More Bible Storybags*® published by BRF 2012 (978 1 84101 836 2) www.barnabasinschools.org.uk

TOGETHER AGAIN (JOSEPH RECONCILED TO HIS BROTHERS)

J collected food when the crops grew well…	*Pile bread*
and he shared the food when the food crops failed.	*Spread bread*
J made the king's land a land of plenty when it could have been a land of hunger.	*Rub stomach*
Far away, the brothers lived in a land of hunger.	*Place brothers*
They heard there was food in the land of plenty.	*Place brothers*
They spoke to J in the land of plenty…	*Place brothers*
but they did not recognise J their brother in the land of plenty…	*Place brothers*
their long-lost brother in the land of plenty	*Place brothers*
until he made it known.	
Then they felt their shame rise.	*Touch cheek*
This was the brother…	*Indicate Joseph*
they had sold as a slave.	
Now he had them in his power.	*Make a fist*
J looked long at his brothers.	*They were shaking with fear.*
J made a choice of what to remember.	
He made a choice to unclasp his hands…	*Open hand*
and clasp his brothers lovingly.	*Move Joseph to brothers*
For he had been part of God's plan.	*Sign 'God'*

Questions

(See also page 11.)

* What caused the brothers' shame?
* Can we decide what we remember?
* Can we decide what we do about the things we remember?

Reproduced with permission from *More Bible Storybags*® published by BRF 2012 (978 1 84101 836 2) www.barnabasinschools.org.uk

TOGETHER AGAIN (JOSEPH RECONCILED TO HIS BROTHERS)

Safe with me

Baby Moses

Using the storybag® in assembly

✂ You will need
* Moses basket or a picture of one

Introduce the assembly by showing the basket and asking what it is called. Today's story is about how the basket got its name and about God working through the love and care of others. Read the Bible story (see page 58). Alternatively, use an online version: www.topmarks.co.uk/judaism/moses/index.htm.

> **Comment**
> This is a story of the love and care of a family. Christians believe that God was there and that he worked through the love and care of the family and the princess. They believe that God still works through people today.

Reflection

Use the storybag® script 1 or 2 as a reflection. It can be read by the teacher with pupils performing any gestures, sign language or sounds. Pupils can also hold up objects and people from the bag. PowerPoint visuals of the story cloths can be accessed via www.barnabasinschools.org.uk/cooling2.

Prayer (optional)

Christ has no body now on earth but ours, no hands but ours, no feet but ours. Ours are the eyes through which Christ's love looks out to the earth, ours are the feet by which he is to go about doing good and ours are the hands by which he blesses others now.

Teresa of Avila (adapted)

Introduce the subject using some of the material from the assembly introduction (see page 57). On the same page you will find a comment on the biblical story. Select the appropriate script and turn to pages 9 and 10 to find ways of using it.

Biblical material

Exodus 2:1–10

The king of Egypt feared his Israelite slaves; they could be trouble if they turned against him, so he worked them so hard that they were too tired to do anything but survive. Despite his cruelty, despite all the hard work, the Israelite people not only survived but also had children and grew in number. The king was angry and sent out his soldiers, who were cruel and ruthless. The people hid from the soldiers in fear, hoping they would pass by.

In one family a baby was born, a little boy, and the whole family kept him hidden because the king's soldiers were everywhere. The mother placed the baby boy in a waterproof basket, like a little boat, and hid it in the tall grass by the edge of the river. The baby's sister, Miriam, kept watch over the basket to make sure her brother was safe. As she watched, a princess came to the river to bathe. As she washed, the baby began to cry. The princess found the basket and was surprised to find a baby inside. She decided to keep him. 'I shall call him Moses, but I shall need someone to help me care for him.'

Miriam heard what the princess said and went to her. 'My mother will help you. Shall I bring her to you?'

'Yes,' replied the princess, 'go and fetch her and I will pay her to look after him.'

Miriam brought her mother to the princess and soon the family were together again. When Moses was older, he went to live at the palace. God had a special job for Moses. One day he would help his people—but that is another story.

Follow-up activities

Select from the activities below, according to the age and aptitude of your pupils. (See also pages 11 and 12.)

1. Create a two-dimensional display of this story that reflects the layout of the bag. Add two-dimensional versions of items from the story. Place the appropriate story script and an open children's Bible on a table. Add questions and pupils' comments, and use them as a basis for discussion.

2. Draw the scene you like best from the story on a photo-size piece of paper and say why you like it. Put the class photos together to make a photo album. Add captions. Add a star to the photo that you think is the most important, and say why.

3. Imagine you could interview Miriam. What questions would you ask? An adult can play the part of Miriam to respond to the questions for younger pupils.

4. Draw a target diagram. Place a picture of Moses in the basket in the centre. In the next circle, write what you think is the message of this story. In the outside ring, write anything else you think is important to Christians about this story.

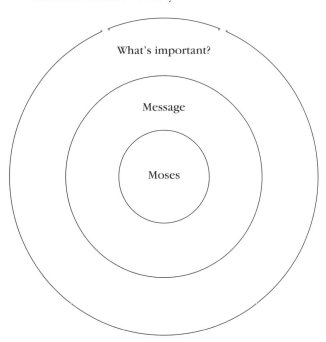

5. In the story, God works through the mother, sister and princess to save Moses. Christians believe that God works through people today. Make a collage of handprints and arrange the prayer of Teresa of Avila (see page 57) around them.

6. Tell the story of Moses silently, using mime, gestures and signing. Record it on video (with permission). Assess the video against the story. How could it be improved? How could the message of the story be communicated in this way?

Symbols used in the story

⊕ Hand: this is used as a symbol of God's power and care in the Bible.

⊕ God: right index finger points upwards at shoulder height, other digits curl inwards.

Signs used in the story (British Sign Language)

⊕ Fear: slightly curled right hand taps chest.

Useful websites

⊕ www.signstation.org (go to the BSL dictionary, then A–Z for the word 'fear')

⊕ www.christiansigns.org.uk (search 'vocab' for the word 'God')

⊕ www.britishsignlanguage.com

Reflective activity

Pass the starter sentence, 'Hands for…' and ask pupils to complete it positively by saying what good things they can use their hands for.

Assessment

Assess the pupils' understanding by observing them replaying the script, or ask them to talk about the display or write about it.

Background information and understanding the story

⊕ The Israelites went to Egypt during the time of Joseph. This family clan multiplied and eventually became the nation of Israel.

⊕ The kings of Egypt (Pharaohs) viewed the Hebrews (also known as Israelites) living on the border as a security risk. The Pharaoh tried to reduce their numbers by making them slaves, overworking them and killing their baby boys by throwing them in the Nile. (This needs handling sensitively and the story has been phrased so as not to be explicit.)

⊕ God is behind the scenes in this story, working through the care of this family. In Script 2, this idea is expressed as God's hand caring for the baby. The Bible talks about God holding people in his hands. This does not mean that God has hands: it is a way of talking about God as caring and powerful. The song 'He's got the whole world in his hands' is another example.

⊕ Babies were breastfed for about three years. During that time, Moses would have lived with his birth family. Moses was adopted by the princess and would have received an Egyptian education. His dual heritage put him in the perfect position to negotiate with the king for the release of the Hebrew slaves when he was older. For Christians, this story is about God's plan to save the Hebrew people.

Useful websites

⊕ www.textweek.com/art/baby_moses.htm (select scripture index for other information)

⊕ www.teachingandlearningresources.co.uk/colourbookmoses.shtml (pictures to download)

⊕ www.jesusandkidz.com/html/j_babymoses_00.htm

⊕ www.biblical-art.com/biblicalsubject2.asp?id_biblicalsubject=1264

You will need

* A yellow bag
* Five people figures (mother, father, sister, baby and princess with gold collar or crown)
* A wide blue ribbon
* Crumpled green tissue for tall grass
* Small card box (open) for basket or a knitted basket and lining (see pages 16–17)

Questions

(See also page 11.)

* Who is surprised in this story? Why?
* Who is happy? When?
* I wonder what job this baby will do.

Script 1

Unpacking the bag

My bag is yellow, the colour of the sun.
There is a river in my bag, wide and deep.
There is grass that grows by the river,
and a princess who bathes there.
There is a family in my bag: mother, father, sister and baby,
and a basket… I wonder what this does.

The story

Our story takes place on a yellow cloth, the colour of the sun *(place bag)*. In a land where the sun is hot and the land is dry, a deep river flows *(place ribbon river)*. Grass grows by the river, tall and thick *(place grass)*.

A family lives in the hot, dry land: mother, father, sister, baby *(place family)*. They are afraid *(sign 'fear')*, for the king is angry and his cruel soldiers are about. They need to keep the baby safe. God *(sign 'God')* is watching over the child, for this baby has a job to do when he grows up. They decide to hide the baby in a basket by the river *(place baby in basket in grass by river)*. His sister stands nearby, keeping watch *(place sister)*.

A princess comes to the river to wash *(place princess)*. She hears the baby's cry and finds him in his basket in the grass *(move princess)*. The princess decides to look after the child but knows she will need help. The sister brings her mother to the princess *(move mother)* and they offer to help look after the baby *(put baby with mother)*. The princess pays the mother to look after the baby, and soon they are all back together again and safe *(put all the family together again)*.

Reproduced with permission from *More Bible Storybags*® published by BRF 2012 (978 1 84101 836 2) www.barnabasinschools.org.uk

SAFE WITH ME (BABY MOSES)

Script 2

Unpacking the bag

My bag is yellow, the colour of the sun.
There is a river in my bag, wide and deep.
There is grass that grows by the river.
There is a family in my bag: mother, father, sister and baby,
and a basket to keep a baby safe.
There is a princess in my bag.

The story

You will need
* A yellow bag
* Five people figures (mother, father, sister, baby and princess with gold collar or crown)
* A wide blue ribbon
* Crumpled green tissue for tall grass
* Small card box (open) for basket or a knitted basket and lining (see pages 16–17)

Our story takes place on a sun-coloured cloth…	*Place cloth*
in a land where a great river flows…	*Place river*
and grass grows tall.	*Place grass*
Long ago in this sun-filled land, the people were afraid.	*Sign 'fear'*
A tiny cry cut the air…	*Place baby on sand*
a baby's cry.	
'Don't cry,' said the mother.	*Place mother near baby*
'Don't cry,' said the father.	*Place father*
'Don't cry,' said the sister.	*Place sister*
'Be quiet, little one…	*Finger on lips*
the soldiers are near.'	
The mother made a basket…	*Place basket*
strong and sealed, shaped like a boat.	
She gently laid the baby there…	*Place baby in basket*
and rocked him.	*Rock basket*
'Don't cry,' the mother said…	*Lift mother*
rocking the basket.	*Rock basket*
'Don't cry,' the father said…	*Lift father*

Reproduced with permission from *More Bible Storybags*® published by BRF 2012 (978 1 84101 836 2) www.barnabasinschools.org.uk

SAFE WITH ME (BABY MOSES)

Older pupils

rocking the basket.	*Rock basket*
'Don't cry,' the sister said…	*Lift sister*
rocking the basket.	*Rock basket*
'The soldiers are near.'	
And the baby was quiet.	*Finger on lips*
The mother hid the basket in the tall grass…	*Place basket in grass*
that grew in the shallow waters of the river.	
The river gently rocked the basket-boat.	*Rock basket*
'Don't cry,' it seemed to say. 'You are safe with me.'	
A princess came down to the river to wash…	*Place princess*
She heard the baby's cry.	
Parting the grasses, she saw the baby lying in his basket-boat.	*Move her to basket*
'Don't cry, little one,' she said. 'You are safe with me, but I need help to care for you.'	
The baby's mother helped with his care…	*Place basket with family*
and they were together again.	
As the mother rocked his cradle…	*Rock cradle*
she sensed another 'hand'. Someone else cared for her child. He was safe.	

Questions

(See also page 11.)

* This is a story about women. How do they outwit the soldiers?
* What was this other 'hand'? Was it a real hand? What might it represent?
* How does the baby end up back safely with his parents?

Reproduced with permission from *More Bible Storybags*® published by BRF 2012 (978 1 84101 836 2) www.barnabasinschools.org.uk

SAFE WITH ME (BABY MOSES)

Let my people go

Moses leads his people to freedom

Using the storybag® in assembly

See the pastoral note on page 64.

Introduce the assembly by auctioning a willing adult. The bids can go as high as you like but do not accept any, because no one is rich enough to buy a person; they are beyond price. Explain that our story is about freeing people who are slaves.

Read the Bible story on page 64. Alternatively, use part of an online version, such as www.topmarks.co.uk/judaism/moses/moses3.htm.

Comment

Moses was a famous person who led the Hebrew slaves to freedom, but Moses was not the only one involved. To risk trusting him, leaving Egypt and crossing the desert took great courage on the part of the Hebrew people. They all had their parts to play.

Reflection

Use the storybag® script 1 or 2 as a reflection. It can be read by the teacher, with pupils performing any gestures, sign language or sounds. Pupils can also hold up objects and people from the bag. PowerPoint visuals of the story cloths can be accessed via www.barnabasinschools.org.uk/cooling2.

Prayer (*optional*)

Father Almighty, you heard the cry of the slaves and led them to freedom through Moses. Hear the cries of those who are oppressed today and strengthen those who work to free them from oppression.

Using the storybag® in RE

Pastoral note: this story refers to the death of the 'firstborn'. The story is worded carefully but teachers need to be aware of it.

Introduce the subject using some of the material from the assembly introduction (see page 63). On the same page you will find a comment on the biblical story. Select the appropriate script and turn to pages 9 and 10 to find ways of using it.

Biblical material

Exodus 2:11—14:31

For the first part of this story, see page 58.

One day, when Moses was grown up, he watched the slaves working. As he watched, an Egyptian started beating a slave—one of Moses' own people. Moses was so upset that he killed the Egyptian. The king heard of what had happened and was angry, so Moses ran away to the desert, where he became a shepherd.

Moses was looking after his sheep in the desert when he saw a bush that looked as if it was on fire but was not being burned up. Moses stepped closer to see what was going on. That was when he heard the voice telling him to take off his shoes, for this was holy ground—a very special place.

God spoke to Moses, saying that he had heard the prayers of his people who were slaves in Egypt, and he told Moses to go back to Egypt and set his people free. Moses did not want to go.

'I'm not a good speaker,' said Moses. 'And who is going to listen to me?'

God gave Moses ways of showing people that God had sent him, but still Moses did not want to go.

God told Moses he would be with him and would give him the words to say. Moses' brother, Aaron, would also help.

'Who shall I say has sent me?' asked Moses.

'Say that the Lord, whose name is "I AM", sent you—the God of their fathers.'

Moses left the desert and began the long journey to Egypt. In Egypt he came before the king and asked the king to let the people go. The king said 'no' and became so angry that he made the slaves work even harder. Moses felt bad; he had just made things worse. 'Don't worry,' said God. 'Things will change.'

Ten times Moses asked the king to let the people go. He warned the king that terrible things would happen to the Egyptian people if he said 'no'. Ten times the king said 'no' and each time something terrible happened and the people of Egypt suffered: the rivers turned to blood, then there were frogs everywhere, and then tiny buzzing gnats. Still the king said 'no'. The gnats were followed by flies, then the animals became ill and the people got sores. Still the king said 'no'. Then there was hail that flattened the crops, and locusts that ate all the food, and a great darkness over the land. Still the king said 'no'.

Moses begged the king to let the slaves go to avoid more suffering. He warned of a terrible tragedy to come if the king refused. Still the king said 'no'. There was sadness all over Egypt as each Egyptian family suffered the loss of their eldest boy. During all these frightening and sad times, no harm came to the slaves. In the past, they had been the ones who had suffered.

After the tenth terrible tragedy, the king said 'yes' and the slaves got ready to leave. They ate a special meal to remind them that they had been kept safe and death had passed over their homes. The people left Egypt and had got as far as the sea when the king changed his mind and sent soldiers to bring them back. The people were trapped. The sea was in front of them and the soldiers were behind them. There was nowhere to go. Moses prayed and a great wind blew. The waters parted and the people crossed to safety.

Follow-up activities

Select from the following activities, according to the age and aptitude of your pupils. (See also pages 11 and 12.)

1. Create a wall display of this story that reflects the layout of the bag. Add two-dimensional versions of items from the story. Place the appropriate story script and an open children's Bible on a table. Add questions and pupils' comments, and use them as a basis for discussion.

2. Make a burning bush in different colours and media. On flame shapes add important words from this story. Why are those words important?

3. Imagine you are making this story into a film. Design a DVD cover for it. On the back, write what your film is about and why people should watch it today. What would such a film have to say to people today?

4. If you could talk to Moses, what would you want to say to him? What do you think Moses would say to us?

5. Older pupils could write a poem about the man who was 'nobody' who became 'somebody'. Try the following pattern: Line 1: statement; Line 2: description; Line 3: comment. For example:

   Mr Nobody,
   tending sheep on a desert plain;
   God's 'somebody' in waiting.

6. Research the festival of Passover (see websites listed below) and how it links to this story. Draw a Passover table and add notes about the festival, showing links to the story. Why do you think Jewish people still celebrate this story today?

Symbols used in the story

☷ Fire: symbol of holiness

Signs used in the story (British Sign Language)

☷ 'No': right hand waved across face.
☷ 'God': right hand at shoulder level, right index finger points upward, other digits curled inwards.
☷ Prayer as a conversation with God: palms together in prayer, then open them like a book and move them up and down, with little fingers rubbing against each other.
☷ 'Free': hands at waist height, backs uppermost, horizontal, fingers open, tips of middle fingers almost touching. Raise them to chest height, moving them apart with a sweeping gesture, the backs of the hands turning to face the audience.

Useful websites

☷ www.signstation.org (go to the BSL dictionary, then A–Z for the words 'free' and 'no')
☷ www.christiansigns.org.uk (search 'vocab' for the words 'prayer' and 'God')
☷ www.britishsignlanguage.com

Reflective activity

Make paper chains from loops of paper. Ask pupils, as they add each loop, to think about what the slaves would have appreciated most about their freedom.

Assessment

Assess the pupils' understanding by observing them replaying the script, or ask them to talk about the display or write about it.

Background information and understanding the story

☷ Moses probably felt like a 'nobody' after being an Egyptian prince. Moses' experience in the desert prepared him to lead his people across it later.
☷ The people of Egypt suffered as a result of Pharaoh's refusal. Up to that moment, it had been the slaves and their families who had suffered. (This needs careful handling as the last plague involves the death of children.)
☷ In the story, God says that his name is 'I AM'—the one who just is. The name for God is YAHWEH (pronounced Yah-way), which means 'I am'.

Useful websites

☷ www.primaryresources.co.uk/re/re_Judaism.htm (select as appropriate)
☷ www.holidays.net/passover/seder_plate.htm
☷ www.textweek.com/art/moses.htm (select scripture index for other information)
☷ www.topmarks.co.uk/judaism/moses/moses3.htm
☷ www.teachingandlearningresources.co.uk/ colourbookmoses.shtml (illustrations)
☷ www.textweek.com/art/burning_bush.htm (select scripture index for other information)
☷ www.biblical-art.com/biblicalsubject2.asp?id_ biblicalsubject=1264

Script 1

Unpacking the bag

My bag is desert-coloured.
There are people in my bag: a king and his soldiers.
There are people in my bag: slaves who make bricks.
There is a shepherd in my bag and his sheep.
There is a burning bush, a sea that parts and tears that fall.

The story

In the lonely desert *(place bag)*, a shepherd looked after his sheep *(add shepherd and sheep to one corner of the bag)*.

Far away, his family were slaves—making bricks in the hot, hot sun *(add slaves and bricks on the opposite corner of the bag)*. The slaves cried as they worked and their cries *(add two tears)* were heard in heaven *(sign 'God')*.

Back in the desert, the shepherd saw a bush that flamed with fire *(add bush)* and he turned to watch *(move Moses to bush)*. From the bush, a voice called the shepherd to leave his sheep and go to his people and set them free. 'No!' said the shepherd *(sign 'no')*. 'I'm not good at speaking; no one will listen to me.' 'Go,' said the voice *(point)*. 'I will give you words to say. Set my people free' *(sign 'free')*.

The shepherd left the desert and went to the king *(add king a little distance from slaves)*. 'Set my people free,' said the shepherd. 'No,' said the king *(sign 'no')*. Ten times the shepherd asked *(hold up ten digits, count)* and ten times the king said, 'No' *(sign 'no' together once, hold up ten digits, count)*. Ten times there were tears and sadness *(drop ten tears)* until the king said 'Yes' *(nod)*.

The slaves packed their bags and left with the shepherd *(move people away from king)*, but the king changed his mind and sent his soldiers after them *(place soldiers behind them)*. The slaves reached the sea *(add sea in front of them)* and there was nowhere to go: soldiers behind *(lift soldiers)*, sea in front *(indicate sea)*. The shepherd prayed *(sign 'prayer')* and a great wind blew *(wind noises)*. The sea parted *(pull sea apart)* and they crossed in safety *(move people)*.

You will need

* A bag in desert camouflage or a plain sandy colour
* Lego® bricks
* Six people figures (two slaves, two soldiers, one shepherd and one king with crown)
* Two sheep (from animal set or knitting pattern on page 17)
* Red and yellow or orange tissue for burning bush
* Silver paper tears (about 20)
* Strip of blue fabric or wide blue ribbon cut in two and joined with tape

Questions
(See also page 11.)

* Why do you think the shepherd stopped to look at the bush?
* Whose voice do you think he heard?
* Why didn't the shepherd want to go?

Reproduced with permission from *More Bible Storybags*® published by BRF 2012 (978 1 84101 836 2) www.barnabasinschools.org.uk

LET MY PEOPLE GO (MOSES LEADS HIS PEOPLE TO FREEDOM)

Script 2

Unpacking the bag

My bag is desert-coloured.
There are people in my bag: a king and his soldiers.
There are people in my bag: slaves who make bricks.
There is a shepherd in my bag who thinks he is nobody but used to be somebody.
There is a burning bush, a sea that parts, and many, many tears.

You will need
* A bag in desert camouflage or a plain sandy colour
* Lego® bricks
* Six people figures (two slaves, two soldiers, one shepherd and one king with crown)
* Two sheep (from animal set or knitting pattern on page 17)
* Red and yellow or orange tissue for burning bush
* Silver paper tears (about 20)
* Strip of blue fabric or wide blue ribbon cut in two and joined with tape

The story

Our story takes place on a desert cloth…	*Place cloth*
where a lonely shepherd works.	*Place shepherd*
This shepherd thinks he is nobody…	*Lift shepherd*
but he used to be somebody.	*Replace*
In a land far away, slaves work…	*Place slaves on corner of bag*
making bricks in the merciless sun.	*Add bricks*
Their cries are heard.	*Add a few tears*
Something is about to happen.	
Deep in the desert, a bush burns…	*Add bush*
and the shepherd who thinks he is nobody stops and looks and listens.	*Move shepherd to bush*
'I have heard my people,' says the voice in the bush.	*Sign 'God'*
'I have seen their tears.	*Add more tears*
Set my people free.'	*Sign 'free'*
Then the man who thinks he is nobody shakes his head.	*Shake head*
He can't lead.	*Shake head*
He can't speak.	*Touch lips, shake head*

He is nobody. How could he free the people?	*Sign 'free' and shrug*
The voice speaks on…	*Sign 'God'*
knowing that this man could be a somebody.	*Indicate shepherd*
The man who thinks he is nobody says, 'Yes'…	*Nod head*
turns his back on the desert and walks towards the future…	*Move shepherd*
to set the people free.	*Sign 'free'*
The man who is nobody stands before the king…	*Place king by shepherd*
and begins to feel like somebody.	
'Let my people go,' he says.	
But the king's heart is hard.	*Touch heart*
He will not free the slaves.	*Indicate slaves*
Ten chances.	*Hold up ten digits*
Ten choices.	*Hold up ten digits*
Ten tears: 1, 2, 3, 4, 5, 6, 7, 8, 9, 10.	*Add ten tears*
Ten times the king says, 'No'…	*Sign 'no*
and chooses death over life.	
'No!' 1, 'No!' 2, 'No!' 3, 'No!' 4, 'No!' 5, 'No!' 6, 'No!' 7, 'No!' 8, 'No!' 9, 'No!' 10.	*Hold up correct number of digits*
Finally the king says, 'Yes'…	*Nod head*
and lets the people go.	*Move shepherd and slaves*
Walking to freedom, the people hurry on.	
The king changes his mind and sends his soldiers after them.	*Add soldiers behind slaves*
Behind are soldiers…	*Lift and replace*
in front is the sea.	*Add sea in front of slaves*

Reproduced with permission from *More Bible Storybags*® published by BRF 2012 (978 1 84101 836 2) www.barnabasinschools.org.uk

LET MY PEOPLE GO (MOSES LEADS HIS PEOPLE TO FREEDOM)

The man who had been nobody prays	*Sign 'prayer'*
and he who made the seas…	*Sign 'God'*
parts the waters…	*Separate waters*
and the people walk on.	*Move people*

Questions

(See also page 11.)

✻ How can a person think of themselves as nobody?

✻ What does it mean to be somebody?

✻ Who is the voice in the story?

Reproduced with permission from *More Bible Storybags®* published by BRF 2012 (978 1 84101 836 2) www.barnabasinschools.org.uk

LET MY PEOPLE GO (MOSES LEADS HIS PEOPLE TO FREEDOM)

Cloud and fire

Crossing the desert and the Ten Commandments

Using the storybag® in assembly

You will need
* A large sheet of paper and a pen

Draw a map of your room on the paper and mark a cross on it. Ask one pupil to guide another pupil to the place marked with the cross, using the map you have drawn. Talk with the pupils about finding your way with a map. Today we have satellite navigation systems and all sorts of things to help us find our way.

Today's story is about the Israelites crossing the desert. They had no map but they did have help. Read the Bible story on page 71.

Comment

The Israelites crossed the desert without a map but they had Moses, who had worked in the desert, and the cloud and fire to lead them and to reassure the people that God went with them. Christians believe that God is invisible but sometimes he shows his presence in special ways. The Israelites were probably very frightened about crossing a desert. They had been slaves for a long time and needed to know that they were not alone.

Reflection

Use the storybag® script 1 or 2 as a reflection. It can be read by the teacher, with pupils performing any gestures, sign language or sounds. Pupils can also hold up objects and people figures from the bag. PowerPoint visuals of the story cloths can be accessed via www. barnabasinschools.org.uk/cooling2.

Prayer (optional)

Walk with us through the world, God:
Be before us to guide,
Be beside us to protect,
Be around us to comfort,
Even if we cannot see you.

Introduce the subject using some of the material from the assembly introduction (see page 70). On the same page you will find a comment on the biblical story. Select the appropriate script and turn to pages 9 and 10 to find ways of using it.

Biblical material

Exodus 13:20–22; 15:22—20:21; 24:3–7; 32:1–8;
Numbers 9:15–23; 13:1—14:10

> Earlier episodes in the story of Moses can be found on pages 58 and 64.

The Israelites had been slaves in Egypt, but God had used Moses to free them. They left Egypt and slavery behind and Moses led them into the desert. A thick cloud went with them during the day, which was lit up by fire at night. The cloud led the way and showed them that God was with them.

The desert was long and hard and the people started moaning: they needed food and fresh water, and each of these God supplied. He sent great flocks of birds that flew low so that people could catch them to eat. In the mornings a strange food like flakes covered the ground. It was sweet and good to eat. The people did not know what to call it, so they called it 'manna', which means 'What is it?'

The journey was eventful. At one point they were attacked by enemies and had to defend themselves; they were only slaves and were not used to fighting, so they needed God's help to win the battle. Eventually, the people reached the mountain called Sinai. Thunder and lightning covered the mountain and the people were afraid. Moses went up the mountain and God spoke to him there and gave Moses laws for the people to live by. These laws were special: they showed people how to live in peace with God and each other.

1. Worship God alone.
2. Do not worship idols.
3. Use God's name carefully.
4. Keep the sabbath day as a special day.
5. Respect your father and your mother.
6. Don't murder.
7. Keep your wedding promises to your husband or wife.
8. Don't steal.
9. Don't tell lies.
10. Don't always be wanting what others have.

God made an agreement with the Israelites: they would worship only God and keep his laws, and he would be their God. Unfortunately, the Israelites were not good at keeping this agreement or God's laws, but God did not give up on them. On God's instructions the Israelites made a very, very special tent, which they carried through the desert so that they had a place to worship God. The people left the mountain and moved on, with the cloud before them by day and fire by night.

Time went by and the people travelled on. Once again they began moaning: 'We're fed up with manna—the food was better in Egypt!' Once again God sent the birds that were easy to catch. Finally, the people got to Canaan and Moses sent twelve men to see what the land was like. The men cut a great bunch of grapes to show how good the food was, but when they saw the people and the cities with big, high walls, their hearts sank. The men came back and reported that the land was good but the people were strong and scary and the towns had huge walls. Ten of the men said there was no way they could take this land. Two men thought differently: they thought they could do it with God's help.

The Israelites were frightened and decided not to try to enter the land. As a result, God kept them in the wilderness until a new generation had grown up who were ready to go into the land.

Follow-up activities

Select from these activities, according to the age and aptitude of your pupils. (See also pages 11 and 12.)

1. Create a two-dimensional display of this story that reflects the layout of the bag. Add two-dimensional versions of items from the story. Place the appropriate story script and an open children's Bible on a table. Add questions and pupils' comments, and use them as a basis for discussion.

2. Create a desert 'train line'. As a class, design the story of the crossing of the desert as a railway journey with different events happening at different 'stations': leaving Egypt, food and water, attack by enemies and so on. Give the stations names to reflect the events—for example, 'Sinai junction'. Add pupils' accounts of events. Younger pupils can arrange prewritten accounts of events along a railway journey line. The events can be enacted as pupils 'journey' along the line. Pupils can discuss in what ways our lives are like a journey.

3. In art, create cloud and fire images using different media. Add text to the image in some way to make the link to God. Older pupils can design a symbol for Christians today to indicate that God is near.

4. Tell the story in a series of speech and thought bubbles. Intersperse the speech bubbles with 'Are we there yet?' To do this, you will need to discuss the story and decide what people would be saying and thinking at different points in the story. Christians reading this story will ask themselves what it has to say to them. What do you think they might take from this story to help them to live as Christians?

5. List the Ten Commandments (see page 71). Take the commandment on stealing and discuss what it would mean for self, others and society (SOS) if everyone obeyed it. Ask pupils for their ideas on what helps people to obey laws. Why do some people break this law?

6. In what ways could a law be a gift? Arrange one law as a gift—for example, mount it on gift-wrapping paper. Underneath, write how that law could be a gift to people.

Symbols used in the story

☉ Cloud: a bright cloud was an image of God's presence and glory.
☉ Fire: fire is associated with God; its purifying aspect relates to God's holiness.

Signs used in the story (British Sign Language)

☉ 'God': right hand at shoulder level, right index finger points upward, other digits curled inwards.
☉ 'Moan': right hand, press fingers and thumb together and release as you draw your hand away from your mouth. Repeat.
☉ 'Sad': right hand held vertically in front of the face, side on. Move do1wn to just below the chin.
☉ 'Fear': right hand, fingers slightly curled, tap chest.

Useful websites

☉ www.signstation.org (go to the BSL dictionary, then A–Z for the words 'moan' and 'fear')
☉ www.christiansigns.org.uk (search 'vocab' for the word 'God')
☉ www.britishsignlanguage.com (for the word 'sad')

Reflective activity

Light a candle. A flame is often lit in churches as a reminder of God's presence. Play some music quietly and ask pupils to consider why a lit candle is used as a symbol of God.

Assessment

Assess pupils' understanding by observing them replaying the script, or ask them to talk about the display or write about it.

Background information and understanding the story

☉ The Israelites crossed the desert by the long route, down the Sinai Peninsula, then up and into Canaan (Israel) from the east (modern Jordan). The quick coastal route to the modern-day Gaza strip was heavily fortified and was also occupied by the Philistines.
☉ The Israelites spent 40 years in the desert until there was a generation that was willing to obey God and ready to enter Canaan. The desert years were not one long march: the people sometimes stayed in an area for some time before moving on.
☉ The Ten Commandments are only ten of many laws in the Old Testament. Jewish believers see the law as a gift, not a restriction (except on wrongdoing). The law is described in the Bible as light, honey and gold.

Useful websites

☉ www.textweek.com/art/moses.htm (select scripture index for other information)
☉ www.topmarks.co.uk/judaism/commandments/tencomms.htm
☉ www.topmarks.co.uk/judaism/moses/moses9.htm
☉ www.biblical-art.com/biblicalsubject? asp?id_biblicalsubject=1264

Script 1

Unpacking the bag

My bag is the colour of a desert.
There is a cloud in my bag, and fiery fire.
There are people in my bag, and a man who leads them.
There are chains in my bag, a reminder of slavery,
and thunder on a mountain.
There is a scroll in my bag with laws to live by.

The story

Our story takes place on a desert cloth, for this is a story of crossing the desert *(place bag)*. The people had been slaves *(add three people and chains)*, but now they were free and leaving the land of slavery *(remove chains)*. The people followed their leader into the desert *(add Moses, move people)*. A bright cloud went before them by day *(add cloud)* and fire by night *(add fire)* to show that God was there and to show the way. The desert was hard: hot by day *(wipe forehead)*, cold by night *(shiver)*, and the people moaned *(sign 'moan')*. God gave them food and water on the long, long journey but still the people moaned *(sign 'moan')*.

The people travelled on *(move cloud and fire; move people)* with God going before them. Finally, they came to a mountain *(bunch cloth)*. There was thunder over the mountain and the people were afraid *(make thunder noise)*. The leader climbed the mountain *(move leader)* and spoke to God *(sign 'God')*. God gave the people laws to live by *(place scroll)*. The people promised to keep the law and God promised to be their God *(sign 'God')*.

The people travelled on with their new laws for living *(move cloud and fire, move people)* and God went with them. They came to the land that God had promised and sent people to look around *(move two people ahead of the rest)*. They returned with tales of good food growing there, but also of big, big people and big, big towns with big, big walls *(use hands for 'big')*. The people were afraid *(sign 'fear')* and would not go into the land *(move people back a little)*. They stayed in the desert for many, many years until children grew up who were ready to go into the land with God *(sign 'God')*.

You will need

* A bag in desert camouflage or a plain sandy colour
* Four people figures (three Israelites and one Moses)
* White tissue for cloud
* Red tissue for fire
* Tin tray for thunder
* Loops of paper made into a chain
* Paper scroll tied with a ribbon and the word 'LAW' written on the outside

Questions

(See also page 11.)
* Why do you think the people moaned?
* The people had travelled a long time to get to the land. Why didn't they go in?
* How did the people know God was with them in the story?

Reproduced with permission from *More Bible Storybags®* published by BRF 2012 (978 1 84101 836 2) www.barnabasinschools.org.uk

Script 2

You will need

* A bag in desert camouflage or a plain sandy colour
* Four people figures (three Israelites and one Moses)
* White tissue for cloud
* Red tissue for fire
* Tin tray for thunder
* Loops of paper made into a chain
* Paper scroll tied with a ribbon and the word 'LAW' written on the outside

Unpacking the bag

My bag is the colour of a desert.
There is a cloud in my bag, and fire that glows by night.
There are people in my bag, and a man who leads them.
There are chains in my bag, a reminder of slavery.
There is thunder on a mountain.
There is a scroll in my bag with laws to live by.

The story

Our story takes place on a desert cloth…	*Place bag*
for this is the story of a man…	*Place Moses*
the people he led through the desert…	*Place people*
and the one who went with them.	*Sign 'God'*
Slavery behind them…	*Add chains*
the people walked on…	*Move people*
and the one went with them:	*Sign 'God'*
cloud by day, fire by night.	*Place cloud and fire*
The desert was long.	*Indicate desert*
The desert was hard. They forgot the slavery…	*Lift chains*
forgot the sadness…	*Sign 'sad'*
and could see only desert…	*Indicate desert*
and the hardness of now.	
Cloud by day, fire by night…	*Move cloud and fire*
the one went with them…	*Sign 'God'*
providing for their needs.	
Thunder on a mountain…	*Make thunder, bunch cloth*

Reproduced with permission from *More Bible Storybags*® published by BRF 2012 (978 1 84101 836 2) www.barnabasinschools.org.uk

CLOUD AND FIRE (CROSSING THE DESERT AND THE TEN COMMANDMENTS)

the people stood in wonder.	*Circle people round mountain, not touching it*
The man climbed the mountain top…	*Place man on mountain*
to meet the holy one.	
Cloud by day, fire by night…	*Move cloud and fire on to mountain*
the one was with them…	*Sign 'God'*
gifting them the Law.	*Place scroll*
Mountain behind them…	*Flatten mountain*
the people walked on.	*Move people on to cloth*
Cloud by day, fire by night…	*Move cloud and fire*
They came to the land…	*Move to edge of cloth*
but did not obey because they were afraid.	*Sign 'fear'*
They stayed in the desert…	*Move people back to the centre*
until they had learned.	
Cloud by day, fire by night…	*Move cloud and fire*
the one went with them…	*Sign 'God'*

through the desert years, until it was time to enter the land.

Questions
(See also page 11.)

* What do you think the cloud and fire are in the story?
* Do hardships we may be experiencing now make us forget the good times of the past?
* In what ways could law be a gift?
* What do you think the people learned?

Reproduced with permission from *More Bible Storybags*® published by BRF 2012 (978 1 84101 836 2) www.barnabasinschools.org.uk

CLOUD AND FIRE (CROSSING THE DESERT AND THE TEN COMMANDMENTS)

Facing the wall

Joshua and the battle of Jericho

Using the storybag® in assembly

You will need

* Some empty cardboard boxes

Introduce the assembly by asking pupils to help you build a wall from the boxes. The wall creates a barrier. Talk with the pupils about some of the things that are barriers in life. We might come up against things that we feel are too hard for us, or too scary. (Give examples appropriate to your school.) For example, facing a test or doing something for the first time can be scary. Write some of these ideas on the bricks of the wall.

Today's story is about facing challenges. Read the Bible story on page 77.

Comment

This story is all about facing difficulties. The people were frightened when they entered the land of Canaan and saw the size of the city walls. How were they supposed to get pass these cities or defeat them? They were not a trained army and these walls were just enormous. The people learned that trust in God and prayer helped them face this particular challenge.

Reflection

Use the storybag® script 1 or 2 as a reflection. It can be read by the teacher, with pupils performing any gestures, sign language or sounds. Pupils can also hold up objects and people from the bag. PowerPoint visuals of the story cloths can be accessed via www.barnabasinschools.org.uk/cooling2.

Prayer (*optional*)

Lord, there are many barriers in life: walls of difficulty, walls of scary things, walls of things that can stop us in our tracks. When we face walls of difficulty, teach us to talk to you (pupils remove some bricks). When we face walls of scary things, remind us to trust you (pupils remove more bricks). When we face things that stop us in our tracks, teach us to support each other to face the challenges life brings (pupils remove last bricks).

Introduce the subject using some of the material from the assembly introduction (see page 76). On the same page you will find a comment on the biblical story. Select the appropriate script and turn to pages 9 and 10 to find ways of using it.

Biblical material

Joshua 5:13–15; 6:1–20

The people had left Egypt many years before. They were tired of walking, for they had walked across the desert for many years. They were now ready to enter the land God had promised, a land called Canaan. Joshua led the people into the land and they were glad that the long journey was almost over. Then they saw the great cities of Canaan with massive walls around them. With fear in their hearts, they carried on marching towards the great city walls of Jericho.

Joshua looked at the walls in the distance. His people did not stand a chance, but God thought differently. God spoke to Joshua and gave Joshua a battle plan that seemed very strange. Joshua and the people had to trust him. The people followed God's battle plan. They marched round the wall once a day for six days without saying a word. The only sound was of the priests blowing the trumpets. On the seventh day they marched seven times with the priests blowing the trumpets, then they all gave a great shout and the walls fell down. Jericho was theirs.

Follow-up activities

Select from the activities below, according to the age and aptitude of your pupils. (See also pages 11 and 12.)

1. Create a two-dimensional display of this story that reflects the layout of the bag. Add two-dimensional versions of items from the story. Place the appropriate story script and an open children's Bible on a table. Add questions and pupils' comments, and use them as a basis for discussion.

2. Use untuned instruments and drama to enact this story. Stop the action at different points and freeze-frame: tell the pupils to freeze, ask some pupils to tell you what they are thinking and feeling while in character, and restart the action.

3. Create a TV book for the story of Joshua and Jericho. Draw a TV screen on a sheet of A5 paper. Cut slits at each side of the screen and cut a strip of paper to be pulled through the slits. The paper should be divided into three sections, each the size of the screen, plus extra paper to hold at each end. Pupils can draw the story on the three sections, picking out the most important moments. Discuss their choices and why these moments are important. Older pupils can write a justification.

4. Ask pupils to rewrite the story of the fall of Jericho, bringing out the trust involved. Share the stories and create a class story by combining parts of the pupils' stories. Print the resulting story in very large print. An optional activity is to cut up the story, paste it on to paper bricks and reassemble as a wall. Add to the display.

5. Sometimes we face great obstacles in life. What helps us when facing these 'walls'? Discuss this with pupils and talk about going to people they know and trust, developing perseverance, praying if they have a faith, and so on. As a result of the discussion, create a wall of words and phrases that describe some obstacles. Write them on paper bricks. On the other side of the bricks, write what helps us to face and overcome obstacles.

6. Play some trust games. Talk about whom we trust and the criteria for trust. Discuss the trust and other feelings in the story. What does the story tell us about how the people felt about God? Write up the results of the discussion on trumpet shapes and add to the display.

Symbols used in the story

❂ The wall: in this story the wall is a symbol of pride and complacency. It also stands for all the barriers that the people face in life.

Signs used in the story (British Sign Language)

❂ 'Fear': right hand, fingers slightly curled, tap chest.
❂ 'God': right hand at shoulder level, right index finger points upward, other digits curled inwards.

Useful websites

❂ www.signstation.org (go to the BSL dictionary, then A–Z for the word 'fear')
❂ www.christiansigns.org.uk (search 'vocab' for the word 'God')
❂ www.britishsignlanguage.com

Reflective activity

Make a cardboard box wall and ask pupils to think about times when they have faced hard things and have overcome them. Knock the wall down.

Assessment

Assess the pupils' understanding by observing them replaying the script, or ask them to talk about the display or write about it.

Background information and understanding the story

- Moses had led the people out of Egypt, but he died before entering Canaan. Joshua led the people into Canaan, taking many walled cities such as Jericho. The Israelites needed to conquer Jericho as its army could attack them from the rear if they just went round it.
- Canaan was made up of lots of walled towns like Jericho; it was not a single nation. Canaanites worshipped gods such as Baal. The immorality and cruelty involved in that worship is given as a reason for losing their right to the land.
- The end of this story has been omitted as it involves many deaths. Christians read the Old Testament in light of the New Testament, with Jesus' emphasis on love and forgiveness.

Useful websites

- www.textweek.com/art/joshua.htm
  (search the scripture index for other information)
- www.biblical-art.com/biblicalsubject2.asp?id_
  biblicalsubject=4
- http://gardenofpraise.com/bibl11s.htm jigsaw

Script 1

Unpacking the bag

My bag is brick-coloured, the colour of a wall.
There are people in my bag who stand for an army.
There are bricks in my bag that make a wall.
There is a trumpet in my bag that makes a loud noise.

Story

Our story takes place on a brick-coloured bag, for this is a story of a wall *(place cloth)*. The wall stands tall in the middle of the land *(build a circular brick wall and continue while you say the next few sentences)*. The wall is old and the wall is high. The wall is wide and the wall is thick. The wall was built long, long ago and it stands proud and strong in the middle of the land. The wall sends a message to all around: 'You can't get over me.' So this is the wall: a high wall, a wide wall, a strong wall *(indicate each phrase with hands and arms)*.

The people were marching, marching, marching *(march people, two in each hand, around the edge of the cloth)*. They had marched *(pupils make marching sounds with their hands on the floor while you speak and march the people)* for days, they had marched for weeks, they had marched for months and they had marched for years *(stop people in front of the wall)*. The wall just laughed, 'You won't get past me.'

The leader stopped and the leader listened *(cup ear)*, then he spoke to the people, who followed the plan. The people started marching once again. They marched *(march people, pupils make marching sounds as before)* round the city and said not a word *(make shh sound)*, but some blew trumpets that shattered the silence *(teacher blows trumpet)*.

At first the wall laughed *(draw a smile in the air)* as the people marched in silence *(march people)*, then the wall frowned *(draw downturned mouth in air)* as the marching went on *(march people)*. The marching went on and on and on *(keep marching)* until, on the last day, the trumpets sounded *(teacher blows toy trumpet)*. The people gave a shout and the wall fell down *(push wall over)*.

You will need

* A brick-coloured bag
* Children's wooden or plastic bricks
* Four people figures
* Safe toy trumpet (for the teacher)

Questions
(See also page 11.)
* How do you think the people felt when they saw the wall?
* Who do you think the leader listened to?
* Why was the wall unhappy?

Reproduced with permission from *More Bible Storybags*® published by BRF 2012 (978 1 84101 836 2) www.barnabasinschools.org.uk

FACING THE WALL (JOSHUA AND THE BATTLE OF JERICHO)

Older pupils

You will need

* A brick-coloured bag
* Children's wooden or plastic bricks
* Four people figures
* Safe toy trumpet

Script 2

Unpacking the bag

My bag is brick-coloured, the colour of a wall.
There are people in my bag who stand for an army.
There are bricks in my bag that make a wall.
There is a trumpet in my bag that makes a loud noise.

Story

Our story takes place on a brick-coloured bag…	*Place bag and smooth*
for this is the story of a wall.	*Build circular wall*
The wall stood tall in the middle of the land.	*Build circular wall*
It's a wall that encircled an ancient town…	*Build circular wall*
built by people long, long ago.	*Build circular wall*
A high wall…	*Indicate with hands*
a wide wall…	*Indicate with hands*
a thick wall…	*Indicate with hands*
a strong wall.	*Indicate with arm muscles*
It stood high and mighty…	*Indicate with hands*
in the middle of the land.	
The wall cast its shadow on the people down below…	*Put people at the base of the wall*
who shrank in its shadow and shook with fear.	*Sign 'fear'*
The people were tired.	*March people, two in each hand*
They had been a lifetime marching.	*Pupils use their hands on the floor to make a marching sound*
They had marched across deserts…	*Pupils use their hands on the floor to make a marching sound*

Reproduced with permission from *More Bible Storybags®* published by BRF 2012 (978 1 84101 836 2) www.barnabasinschools.org.uk

FACING THE WALL (JOSHUA AND THE BATTLE OF JERICHO)

they had marched over mountains…	*Bunch cloth, march people*
they had marched across plains…	*Flatten cloth, march people*
and now they stood still, stopped by a wall.	*Stop the marching*
The one above spoke and the leader listened.	*Sign 'God'*
'March!' said the leader and the people started marching…	*Move people round wall*
left, right, left, right…	*Move people round wall*
marching without words.	*Finger on lips*
Only the trumpet cut the dreadful silence.	*Blow trumpet*
The wall above laughed…	*Smile, draw smile with finger in the air*
at the sound of marching.	*Pupils make marching sound with hands*
The wall above frowned…	*Frown, draw downturned mouth in the air*
as the marching went on.	*Make marching sound with hands*
The wall above shook…	*Make marching sound with hands*
as they carried on marching…	*Make marching sound with hands*
until, with a shout, it fell down.	*Knock down wall, blow trumpet*
The wall lay scattered at the feet of the people.	*Turn a brick over*
The people were thankful.	*Smile as before*
They stood safe and secure.	
They had faced the wall, even though they trembled.	*Sign 'fear'*
They had trusted the one…	*Sign 'God'*
even though they shook…	*Sign 'fear'*
and the wall came tumbling down.	*Move some fallen bricks*

Questions
(See also page 11.)
* This wall has a character, like a person. How would you describe that character?
* Why did the people follow this unusual battle plan?
* What do you think went through the marchers' minds as they marched?

Reproduced with permission from *More Bible Storybags*® published by BRF 2012 (978 1 84101 836 2) www.barnabasinschools.org.uk

FACING THE WALL (JOSHUA AND THE BATTLE OF JERICHO)

The cord

The story of Ruth

Using the storybag® in assembly

> ✄ **You will need**
> * Three lengths of different-coloured thick wool about a metre long
> * One extra strand—if possible, sparkly or brightly coloured

See the pastoral note on page 83.

Introduce the assembly by demonstrating, with pupils' help, how three lengths of wool can be twisted into one cord to make it strong (do not use the sparkly or brightly coloured strand). Today's story is about friendship and family. Read the Bible story on page 83.

Comment
Ruth's story is about how family and friends can help each other through good times and bad. The love and care that binds families and friends together is likened to a three-stranded cord in the Bible.

Reflection

Use the storybag® script 1 or 2 as a reflection. It can be read by the teacher, with pupils performing any gestures, sign language or sounds. Pupils can also hold up objects and people figures from the bag. PowerPoint visuals of the story cloths can be accessed via www. barnabasinschools.org.uk/cooling?

Prayer (*optional*)

Unwind the cord, add a fourth strand and wind it up again.

Through the good times and the bad, through the sadness and the joy, you are always there, Lord. You are the strongest strand in the cord that holds us. Teach us that we are part of a cord of care that supports others, and help us to play our part in that care.

Using the storybag® in RE

Introduce the subject using some of the material from the assembly introduction (see page 82). On the same page you will find a comment on the biblical story. Select the appropriate script and turn to pages 9 and 10 to find ways of using it.

> **Pastoral note:** The story of Ruth includes the death of several members of the family. This element is not dwelt on, but teachers will need to decide whether it is appropriate for their class, in light of their pupils' circumstances.

Biblical material

Ruth 1:1—4:17

Naomi and her family lived in the town of Bethlehem. Life was hard for the family, as there was very little food to eat. So they decided to leave their home and find another country where there was food. After a long walk, they came to a country called Moab where there was food, so they decided to stay. They lived in Moab for many years. The boys grew up and married girls from Moab. One was called Orpah and the other was called Ruth.

Sadly, Naomi's husband died and, after some time, the boys died too, so the women were left on their own. Naomi heard that there was food in Bethlehem now, so she packed her bags, ready to go home. She tried to send Ruth and Orpah back to their families, as life would be hard in Bethlehem for Ruth and Orpah; they would be strangers there.

Orpah went back to her parents, though she did not want to leave Naomi, but Ruth refused to go. 'Don't make me go,' said Ruth. 'Where you go, I will go; your people will be my people; your God will be my God. I swear that nothing shall separate us two as long as we live.'

Naomi gave up trying to persuade her, and the two walked all the way to Bethlehem. When they arrived, Naomi told the people what had happened and how Ruth had come to look after her. Ruth worked in the fields, picking up the grain that the cutters dropped. She picked up enough to make sure she and Naomi never went hungry.

One day, the farmer, Boaz, saw how hard Ruth worked and he told his workers to drop some extra grain for her. Boaz looked after Ruth and in time they got married. Ruth and Boaz had a baby boy called Obed, who later became the grandfather of King David.

Follow-up activities

Select from the activities below, according to the age and aptitude of your pupils. (See also pages 11 and 12.)

1. Create a two-dimensional display of this story that reflects the layout of the bag. Add two-dimensional versions of items from the story. Place the appropriate story script and an open children's Bible on a table. Add questions and pupils' comments, and use them as a basis for discussion.

2. Imagine a film was being made of the story. Think up a title and create an advert or poster for it. Communicate what is important about the story for modern viewers. What sort of story is it—a romance, a thriller?

3. Write a recipe for the story. Include the following: important characters, objects and places, beliefs and ideas, feelings and events. Write in the style of a recipe: 'To make a story of Ruth, you will need…'

4. Explore a range of paintings of Ruth (see websites listed on page 84). What different insights does each painting bring? Which painting would you choose to hang at school? Why? Why should someone look at your chosen painting? What is the message of your chosen painting for today?

5. The Bible describes friendship as a three-stranded cord:

   'You are better off to have a friend than to be all alone, because then you will get more enjoyment out of what you earn. If you fall, your friend can help you up. But if you fall without having a friend nearby, you are really in trouble. If you sleep alone, you won't have anyone to keep you warm on a cold night. Someone might be able to beat up one of you, but not both of you. As the saying goes, "A rope made from three strands of cord is hard to break"' (Ecclesiastes 4:9–12).

   Discuss this as a description of the story of Ruth. How are friendship and commitment to others like a cord? Pupils can make colourful cords from twisting three short strands of wool together. Mount these cords, with an explanation of the verses.

6. Using the following weblinks, compare two versions of Ruth's promise to Naomi (Ruth 1:16–17).

   www.biblegateway.com/passage/?search=Ruth%20 1.16-17&version=KJV.

   www.biblegateway.com/passage/?search=Ruth%20 1.16-17&version=MSG.

   Which one communicates the meaning best? What could have been the consequences for Ruth's life of making this promise?

7. See www.bible4schools.org (listed opposite) for PowerPoints, activities and audio stories relating to Ruth.

Symbols used in the story

- Three-stranded cord: a symbol of friendship, love and other invisible things that bind us together for mutual benefit.

Signs used in the story (British Sign Language)

- 'Hope': index and middle fingers crossed at chest level.
- 'Friend': right hand curled over curled left hand at chest height.
- 'Sad': right hand held vertically in front of the face, side on. Move downward to just below the chin.
- 'Happy': with right palm above left palm, make a sliding clap movement.

Useful websites

- www.signstation.org (go to the BSL dictionary, then A–Z for the words 'hope', 'friend' and 'happy')
- www.christiansigns.org.uk (search 'vocab' for alternative signs for the word 'hope')
- www.britishsignlanguage.com (for the word 'sad')

Reflective activity

Give pupils three short strands of wool to twist quickly into a cord to stick into their books. As they look at the colours, ask them to think of whom the strands may represent for them: friends, family and so on. For some, one strand might represent God.

Assessment

Assess the pupils' understanding by observing them replaying the script, or ask them to talk about the display or write about it.

Background information and understanding the story

- The book of Ruth is set not long after the Israelites had settled in Canaan (Israel), possibly in the twelfth century BC. Ruth was the great-grandmother of King David. Although Ruth was not Jewish, by her actions she showed how faith should be lived.
- Ruth was a gleaner who picked up the bits of grain that other workers dropped. Biblical law did not allow farmers to pick up anything that dropped, as this was left for those in need.
- At the end of Ruth's promise (Ruth 1:6–17) is a vow in which she invokes God's action if she does not keep it. This is an ancient vow: it would probably have been accompanied by a gesture such as a finger drawn across the throat.

Useful websites

- www.bible4schools.org/subject-by-subject/art
- www.bible4schools.org/subject-by-subject/english
- www.textweek.com/art/ruth.htm
  (go to scripture index for other information)
- www.womeninthebible.net/1.13.Ruth.htm
  (details about Ruth)
- http://gardenofpraise.com/bibl13s.htm
  (online jigsaw puzzle)
- www.dltk-bible.com/old_testament/ruth_and_ naomi-index.htm (online jigsaw puzzle and crafts)
- http://commons.wikimedia.org/wiki/Wheat
  (pictures of wheat)
- www.biblical-art.com/biblicalsubject2.asp?id_ biblicalsubject=6 (art)

Script 1

Unpacking the bag

My bag is plain.
There are people in my bag, a family and more: 1, 2, 3, 4, 5, 6, 7, 8.
There is food in my bag for friends and family.

The story

Our story takes place on a plain cloth, but much will happen on it *(place bag)*. Here is a family: mum, dad and two boys *(place Naomi, husband and sons: count together 1, 2, 3, 4)*. They are hungry, very hungry *(rub stomach)*, for there is little food in their town. They decide to leave and go to another country where there is food *(move family)*. After much walking, they come to another country and settle there *(move family)*. While they are there, the family knows happiness when the boys marry two girls from their new country *(add Ruth and Orpah, sign 'happy')*. They also know loss and sadness when the father and the boys die *(remove dad and two boys, sign 'sad')*.

The mother and two girls are left all alone *(bring three women together)*. The mother decides to go home as there is food there now. She packs her bags *(mime)* and tells the girls to go back *(point away to the distance)* to their families, who will look after them. One of the girls goes home *(point)* to her family, though she does not really want to go *(remove Orpah)*. The other girl says she is not leaving, so the two women travel on together *(move two women)*.

The woman and the girl reach the town, and there the girl works in the fields to get food for them *(move the girl away from the mother, add wheat picture)*. The farmer *(add Boaz)* sees how hard she works and helps her get more food *(add another picture of wheat)*.

The farmer and the girl grow close and they marry *(place Boaz next to Ruth)*. The family is happy again *(sign 'happy')* and a little baby is born *(add baby Obed: count 1, 2, 3, 4)*.

You will need

* A plain coloured bag (any colour)
* Seven adult people figures in different colours, or tie strand of coloured wool or ribbon around each one as a belt
* One baby figure (Obed)
* Pictures of wheat (see weblink on page 84)

Questions
(See also page 11.)
* How do you think the family felt, leaving home and going to a strange country?
* Why do you think one of the girls decided she would stay with the mother?
* Why do you think the farmer helped the girl get food?

THE CORD (THE STORY OF RUTH)

Older pupils

You will need
* A plain coloured bag (any colour)
* Seven adult people figures
* One baby figure (Obed)
* Three strands of coloured wool

Unpacking the bag

My bag is plain.
There are people in my bag, friends and family.
There are strands of wool in my bag that twist to make a cord.

The story

Our story takes place on a plain cloth…	*Place cloth*
but much will happen on it.	
This is the story of a cord that cannot be broken.	*Hold up the strands of wool, twist them to make a cord, and pull*
This is the story of a family that faces many of the challenges life brings.	*Place Naomi, husband and two sons*
The family walks the road…	*Move family*
driven by hunger.	*Rub stomach*
These people have little food and little hope.	*Sign 'hope'*
They walk towards a foreign land…	*Move family*
bound together by an invisible cord.	*Hold up the cord*
In the foreign land they find food…	*Touch mouth*
but know loss.	*Remove father*
Still the cord holds.	*Hold up the cord and pull*
They find friendship in the new land.	*Sign 'friend'*
The sons find wives…	*Add Ruth and Orpah*
and the cord holds firm.	*Hold up the cord and pull*
Time passes. The cord is stretched and pulled…	*Pull cord*

Reproduced with permission from *More Bible Storybags®* published by BRF 2012 (978 1 84101 836 2) www.barnabasinschools.org.uk

THE CORD (THE STORY OF RUTH)

for life is hard.

They face more loss…	*Remove two boys*
but still the cord does not break.	*Pull cord*
Three women walk…	*Move women*
without husbands, without sons, with even less hope…	*Sign 'hope'*
but the cord holds them tightly together.	*Pull cord*
The older woman tries to break the cord.	*Pull cord*
one daughter leaves but the other clings tight.	*Remove one person*
The cord holds firm.	*Hold up cord*
Together two women walk on.	*Move women*
Arriving at the town, the young woman works…	*Move Ruth on her own*
in the fields and the farms. In the heat of the day…	*Mop forehead*
she works for food so her friend can eat…	
and the cord holds tight.	*Pull cord*
The farmer sees her working…	*Place Boaz*
stretches out a hand to help, and the cord grows stronger.	*Pull cord*
Kindness turns to marriage.	*Put Ruth and Boaz together*
The young woman walks…	*Walk them both*
the fields and the farms with husband and son…	*Add baby*
held by a cord that has not broken.	*Pull cord*
We are all held by cords that we cannot see.	*Hold up cord*

Questions
(See also page 11.)
* What do you think this invisible cord is?
* Why does the cord not break?
* Why do you think the older woman tried to break the cord?

Reproduced with permission from *More Bible Storybags®* published by BRF 2012 (978 1 84101 836 2) www.barnabasinschools.org.uk

THE CORD (THE STORY OF RUTH)

Big and small

David and Goliath

Using the storybag® in assembly

You will need

✳ Some Russian dolls that fit inside each other, or a box of safe items of different sizes.

See the pastoral note on page 89.

Introduce the assembly by showing the Russian dolls or the box. Ask pupils to find the biggest and the smallest items. Now remove the largest item and ask them to select the biggest and smallest. What we call 'biggest' can change.

Today's story is about getting things into perspective (seeing them properly). Read the Bible story on page 89.

Comment
What we call 'biggest' or 'most powerful' can change, depending on what we look at and what we compare it with. Goliath looked at himself and David and knew he was bigger and more powerful. David looked at himself and Goliath, and then thought about God, and he believed that God was bigger and more powerful than Goliath.

Reflection

Use the storybag® script 1 or 2 as a reflection. It can be read by the teacher, with pupils performing any gestures, sign language or sounds. Pupils can also hold up objects and people figures from the bag. PowerPoint visuals of the story cloths can be accessed via www.barnabasinschools.org.uk/cooling2.

Prayer (optional)

Use the song 'Our God is a great big God' as a prayer as well as a song. (Available online: Jo and Nigel Hemming; copyright © 2001 Vineyard Songs.)

Introduce the subject using some of the material from the assembly introduction (see page 88). On the same page you will find a comment on the biblical story. Select the appropriate script and turn to pages 9 and 10 to find ways of using it.

> **Pastoral note:** Explain that throwing stones is not a way of dealing with bullies. David used an appropriate weapon in a time of war to save his people.

Biblical material

1 Samuel 17:1–49; Psalm 23 (one of David's songs)

David was the youngest boy in his family, so he was sent to look after the sheep while his big brothers joined the Israelite army. Being a shepherd could be a dangerous job, as he had to keep the sheep safe from bears and lions, using his sling and his stick. It was quiet on the hills and David had plenty of time to think and talk to God. David was musical so he turned his thoughts into songs and sang them with only the sheep to hear him.

David's older brothers were far away, fighting a war against the Philistines, who had attacked their country. In the Philistine army was a huge soldier called Goliath. He was nearly three metres tall and covered in armour and weapons: he had helmet and shield, body armour, leg armour, sword and spear. Every day, Goliath shouted to the Israelite army, 'Come and fight me! Who is brave enough? If you win, we will be your slaves. If I win, you will be our slaves.' When the Israelites heard Goliath, they hid. No one wanted to fight him.

David went to visit his brothers and, while he was there, he heard Goliath and saw how frightened the Israelite soldiers were. 'Why should my people be afraid?' thought David. 'I must do something about this Goliath.' David went to the king and said he would fight Goliath. The king and his soldiers looked at the size of David and laughed, but they saw that he meant it. 'I have fought lions and bears and I will fight Goliath with God's help,' said David.

David went to fight Goliath, armed with a stick and his sling. Goliath laughed. David carried on walking. 'You come trusting in weapons,' said David. 'I come trusting in God.' This made Goliath angry and he started to attack. David placed a stone in his sling and swung it. The stone hit Goliath on the head and he fell down dead. The people were safe.

Follow-up activities

Select from the activities below, according to the age and aptitude of your pupils. (See also pages 11 and 12).

1. Create a two-dimensional display of this story that reflects the layout of the bag. Add two-dimensional versions of items from the story. Place the appropriate story script and an open children's Bible on a table. Add questions and pupils' comments, and use them as a basis for discussion.

2. Explore the idea of being small on the outside but big on the inside. List the qualities that made David big on the inside. What qualities can we have that make us big on the inside?

3. In pairs, pupils can create a body sculpture of David at a key moment in the story, take a photograph (with permission) and add a caption. One person can be the sculpture and another can be the photographer, then swap places.

4. As a class, decide on the message of the story and create a class version of the story that will communicate it. Arrange the sentences on separate lines. Print the story and jumble the sentences, then ask pupils to arrange them correctly. Evaluate the story. Has it communicated the message?

5. Explore Psalm 23 (one of the psalms of David). What does it say about God and about David's relationship with God? (See www.biblegateway.com/passage/?search=Psalm%2023&version=CEV.)

6. David is often seen as a biblical hero. As a class, discuss what makes a hero and find examples of modern heroes who fulfil some of these criteria. How can ordinary people be heroes? We may not face Goliaths but many people face Goliath-sized challenges in life.

Signs used in the story (British Sign Language)

- ✪ 'God': right hand, shoulder height, index finger pointing upwards.
- ✪ 'Stupid': right hand held in a fist, hits palm of left hand at chest height

- 'Big': with hands at chest level, palms facing, draw them apart.
- 'Small': with hands at chest level, palms facing slightly curved, draw them in.

Useful websites

- www.signstation.org (go to the BSL dictionary, then A–Z for the words 'big', 'small' and 'stupid')
- www.christiansigns.org.uk (search 'vocab' for the word 'God')
- www.britishsignlanguage.com

Reflective activity

Sign the following, using the signs for 'big' and 'small'. 'Goliath was big on the outside but small on the inside. David was small on the outside but big on the inside— big on trust, big on courage.'

Assessment

Assess the pupils' understanding by observing them replaying the script, or ask them to talk about the display or write about it.

Background information and understanding the story

- David was a young man, not fully grown. This story is one example in the Bible of God using people who are weak to overthrow the powerful.
- David would have used his sling as a shepherd to aim a stone to fall at the side or in front of sheep, in order to stop them straying. The sling was also a weapon. The army of Israel developed sling throwers who could throw right- or left-handed.
- The Philistines settled on the coast of Israel, the modern area of Gaza. The Philistines were a military people, probably of Greek origin. Goliath had a shield carrier: this person may have carried his shield before a battle, but Goliath may have wielded it himself in battle.

Useful websites

- http://commons.wikimedia.org (search by David and Goliath)
- www.textweek.com/art/david.htm (use the scripture index for other information)
- http://gardenofpraise.com/bibl14s.htm (online jigsaw puzzle)
- www.biblical-art.com/biblicalsubject2.asp?id_biblicalsubject=152 (pictures)

Script 1

Unpacking the bag

My bag is soldier-coloured, for this is a story of battle.
There are soldiers in my bag, ready to fight: two different armies.
There is a gigantic soldier who is very strong.
There is a boy in my bag, and his sheep.
He carries his stick and his sling and a few small stones.

The story

Our story takes place on a cloth that soldiers wear, for this is a story of war *(place bag)*. In a land far away lived a shepherd boy *(place David)*, who cared for his sheep *(place sheep)* and sang as he worked on the lonely hills. He carried a stick *(place stick in belt)* and he carried his sling *(place sling in belt)* to keep his sheep safe from the hungry lion *(roar)*, to keep his sheep safe from the hungry bear *(growl, make claws)*.

Away from the hills, his brothers stood, part of an army that was not fighting *(place Israelite soldiers)*. They were afraid of a giant man *(place Goliath)* and his fierce soldiers *(place soldiers)* who wanted them to fight. The shepherd boy went to his brothers *(move David)*, saw the giant man and knew what he must do. 'I'll fight this giant,' the shepherd boy said, and everyone laughed: 'Don't be stupid *(sign 'stupid')*! You are just a boy, and he is a solder of enormous strength.'

The shepherd boy took his stick and his sling and a few small stones *(add stones to the belt)* and got ready for battle. The giant man stood in his strength: armour on his legs, armour on his chest, shield on his arm, helmet on his head, sword by his side *(touch relevant parts of the body)*. The shepherd boy stood all alone with no armour on his legs, armour on his chest, shield on his arm, helmet on his head or sword by his side *(touch relevant parts of the body)*. But he did have a heart that trusted God *(sign 'God')*. 'God who helped me fight the lion *(roar)*, God *(sign 'God')* who helped me fight the bear *(growl, make claws)*, guide my hand *(hold up hand)* when I fight this man.'

The giant soldier moved in close. The shepherd boy took his sling, whirled it round *(whirl arm)* and threw a stone, and the giant fell down dead *(knock over Goliath)*.

You will need

* A bag made from battle camouflage
* Six people figures (a very big man, a small boy, two men of one colour to represent Goliath's army, two men of another colour to represent the Israelite army). The small boy should have a belt (strand of wool) to hold his sling
* Small stones (small felt or paper circles)
* Sheep (from farm set, or use the knitting pattern on page 17)
* Stick (rolled paper)
* Sling (felt or paper and string or wool)

Questions
(See also page 11.)
* How did being a shepherd help the boy fight the gigantic soldier?
* How do you think he felt when the others laughed at him?
* I wonder why the boy said he would fight the giant soldier.

Reproduced with permission from *More Bible Storybags*® published by BRF 2012 (978 1 84101 836 2) www.barnabasinschools.org.uk

You will need

* A bag made from battle camouflage
* Six people figures (a very big man, a small boy, two men of one colour to represent Goliath's army, two men of another colour to represent the Israelite army)
* Five small stones (felt circles)
* Sheep (from farm set, or use the knitting pattern on page 17)
* Stick (rolled paper)
* Sling (felt and string or wool)

Script 2

Unpacking the bag

My bag is soldier-coloured, for this is a story of battle.
There are soldiers in my bag, ready to fight: two different armies.
There is a gigantic soldier who is very strong.
There is a boy in my bag, and his sheep.
He carries his stick and his sling and a few small stones.

The story

Our story takes place on a battle cloth…	*Place cloth*
for this is a story of war.	
In a land long ago, there lived a man…	*Place Goliath*
a giant of a man, a bear of a man…	*Make claw gesture*
fearsome as a lion.	*All roar*
When he stamped, the earth shook.	*Hit floor with flat of hand*
When he roared, the people shook.	*All shake, roar*
He was a sight to see with his armour on…	*Pupils touch the different parts of the body*
armour on his legs, armour on his chest, shield on his arm, helmet on his head, sword by his side. He looked like a tank when he went into battle.	
In a land long ago, there lived a boy…	*Indicate smaller height*
a shepherd boy who cared for his sheep.	*Place David and sheep away from Goliath*
He kept them safe from the bear and the lion…	*Make claws and roar*
with his stick and his sling and a few small stones.	*Place items in David's belt*
He sang as he worked, songs that were prayers to the Lord his God…	*Sign 'God'*
who kept him safe as he cared for his sheep.	

Reproduced with permission from *More Bible Storybags®* published by BRF 2012 (978 1 84101 836 2) www.barnabasinschools.org.uk

BIG AND SMALL (DAVID AND GOLIATH)

Near to the hills where the shepherd boy…	*Point to David*
cared for his sheep to keep them safe, the giant-man came with his men.	*Move Goliath, add his army*
He attacked the people who lived in the land.	*Add Israelites facing them*
The shepherd boy heard his people cry and he saw them shake when the giant roared.	*All roar*
He remembered the bear and the hungry lion and felt at his side for his sling and his stones.	*Touch belt*
'My people are like sheep who need to be saved. All I have is my sling and my stones.	
God who helped me fight the bear…	*Sign 'God'*
God who helped me fight the lion…	*Sign 'God'*
will guide my hand when I fight this man.'	*Hold out hand*
The boy took his sling and went to war.	*Move David nearer Goliath*
The giant-man was a sight to behold…	*Pupils touch the different parts of the body*
armour on his legs, armour on his chest, shield on his arm, helmet on his head, sword by his side. He looked like a tank as he faced the boy.	*Sign 'big'*
The shepherd boy looked very young.	*Turn David to face Goliath. Sign 'small'*
He had no armour as he came to battle…	*Pupils touch the different parts of the body*
no armour on his legs, no armour on his chest, no shield on his arm, no helmet on his head, no sword by his side…	
only his sling, his stick and a few small stones…	*Whirl hand*
and trust in his God, deep in his heart.	*Sign 'God'*
The giant laughed; the giant roared.	*Roar, lift Goliath*

Reproduced with permission from *More Bible Storybags*® published by BRF 2012 (978 1 84101 836 2) **www.barnabasinschools.org.uk**

BIG AND SMALL (DAVID AND GOLIATH)

'They've sent a boy; they've sent a kid, with only a stick and a few small stones.' *Show stones*

'Do you think I'm a dog, do you think I'm a fool? Send a real man to do a man's job. Come here, boy, and meet your end. I'll teach you just how strong I am.' *Point to arm muscles*

The shepherd boy looked at the giant man with… *Pupils touch the different parts of the body*

armour on his legs, armour on his chest, shield on his arm, helmet on his head, sword by his side. This man trusted his own great strength.

'You come at me with sword and with shield… *Lift Goliath*

but I come to you in the name of God… *Sign 'God'*

to protect my people whom you would harm.'

Hearing that, the giant moved in close… *Move closer*

and the boy took his sling and whirled it round. *Whirl arm around head*

The stone hit the giant and down he fell. He hit the ground, stone dead. *Knock over Goliath*

The giant's army saw him fall. *Remove men one by one*

Slowly his army melted away.

The people of the land knew they were safe… *Point to other army*

and together they thanked their God. *Sign 'God'*

Questions

(See also page 11.)

* How do you think the shepherd boy felt when he heard the giant laugh at him?
* How did the shepherd boy's faith in God help him?
* How had being a shepherd helped the boy train for this fight?

Reproduced with permission from *More Bible Storybags*® published by BRF 2012 (978 1 84101 836 2) www.barnabasinschools.org.uk

BIG AND SMALL (DAVID AND GOLIATH)

The chocolate box

Solomon's wisdom

  You will need

✱ Some of King Solomon's sayings paraphrased from the book of Proverbs (see below) in a gift box

- Do whatever you can for people who deserve your help (3:27).
- A gentle answer calms down anger (15:1).
- Pride goes before a fall (16:18).
- Patience is better than fighting (16:32).
- A true friend is always a friend, and families share troubles (17:17).
- Respect and a good reputation are worth more than gold (22:1).
- Don't be glad when your enemies fall (24:17).
- Losing self-control is like a city losing its wall defences (25:28).

Beforehand, hide the gift box containing Solomon's sayings in the hall. Introduce the subject by telling pupils there is treasure hidden in the hall and ask a pupil to try to find it. Use 'warm', 'hot', 'cool', 'cold' to indicate if they are near the treasure or not.

When the box is found, explain that a famous king called Solomon said that wisdom was like treasure. Invite pupils to share some of Solomon's wise sayings from the box. Wisdom is the ability to tell right from wrong and live well towards God and other people.

Today's story is about wisdom. Read the Bible story on page 96.

Comment

The story of Solomon is the story of a wise choice. Solomon showed that there are some things that are worth more than fame and money, power and long life. The ability to tell right from wrong and live well towards God and other people is described as a treasure.

Reflection

Use the storybag® script 1 or 2 as a reflection. It can be read by the teacher, with pupils performing any gestures, sign language or sounds. Pupils can also hold up objects and people figures from the bag. PowerPoint visuals of the story cloths can be accessed via www.barnabasinschools.org.uk/cooling2.

 Prayer (optional)

All-wise God, give us your wisdom as we face the choices life brings. Teach us to know right from wrong and how to live well in the world.

Using the storybag® in RE

Introduce the subject using some of the material from the assembly introduction (see page 95). On the same page you will find a comment on the biblical story. Select the appropriate script and turn to pages 9 and 10 to find ways of using it.

Biblical material

1 Kings 3:5–15

King Solomon was tired and went to bed. That night he dreamed, and in his dream God said that Solomon could ask for anything he wanted. Solomon thought: there were many things he could ask for, but he could only choose one. Solomon was a new king. In fact, he felt like a child trying to rule the people. So Solomon asked for wisdom that would help him tell right from wrong, so that he would know how to rule his people well.

God was pleased with Solomon's choice. He had not asked for long life or riches for himself. He had not asked to get even with his enemies. He had asked for wisdom to help rule his people. Because Solomon had been unselfish, God gave him wisdom and also gave him many of the things he had not asked for: long life, riches and the respect of other people.

Follow-up activities

Select from the activities below, according to the age and aptitude of your pupils. (See also pages 11 and 12.)

1. Create a two-dimensional display of this story that reflects the layout of the bag. Add two-dimensional versions of items from the story. Place the appropriate story script and an open children's Bible on a table. Add questions and pupils' comments, and use them as a basis for discussion.

2. Make a book of wise proverbs from the Bible (page 95 lists some). See the following websites for different types of books that pupils can make.
www.makingbooks.com
www.teachpreschool.org/2010/02/making-books-with-children
Ask pupils which proverb is most helpful for living today. Pupils can also make up their own proverb for living well.

3. Explore art images of this story (see websites listed on page 97). Pupils can choose an important moment from the story to capture in a picture of their own making. Add a frame made from paper and decorate it to imitate sweet wrappers. Ask pupils how they would explain their picture and their frame to someone who did not know the story.

4. Retell the story in hand-mime. As the teacher reads the story, the pupils interpret it in hand-mime while seated. They can use British Sign Language at certain points or use their own signs. Ask pupils to tell you what the message of the story is. Decide on the message as a class. Can the message be mimed or signed?

5. Explore the simile of Solomon's choice being like choosing from a box of chocolates. What choices are we faced with in life, in terms of behaviour and the way we live? How would wisdom help? Pupils can create a mock chocolate box and sweets. On the 'sweets', write some of the choices we have to make about how we live.

6. Wisdom includes the ability to work out what is right and wrong in a situation, and what is the right course of action. How could wisdom help us in daily life?

Symbols used in the story

❂ Chocolate box: a symbol of choice.

Signs used in the story (British Sign Language)

❂ 'God': right hand at shoulder level, right index finger points upwards, other digits curled inwards.
❂ 'Think': right index finger touches right temple, other digits curled inwards.
❂ 'Wise': right thumb moves across right side of forehead in sweeping motion.
❂ 'Enemy': Bang sides of little fingers together, other digits curled inwards.

Useful websites

❂ www.signstation.org (go to BSL dictionary, then A–Z for the words 'think', 'wise' and 'enemy')
❂ www.christiansigns.org.uk (search 'vocab' for the word 'God')
❂ www.britishsignlanguage.com

Reflective activity

Give children a choice of sweets. Use nut- and additive-free ones and supply alternatives for those who cannot eat them. (Check for allergies.) As children make their choices, ask them to think about times when they have made a wise choice about how to behave.

Assessment

Assess the pupils' understanding by observing them replaying the script, or ask them to talk about the display or write about it.

Background information and understanding the story

- Solomon reigned for 40 years (c.970–931BC). He was famous for being wise, but towards the end of his reign he did some very unwise things. Gifts such as wisdom do not guarantee good living; gifts have to be used wisely.
- Under Solomon, Israel reached its peak of power and wealth. The borders of Israel spread to their greatest extent and trade expanded. Solomon was a great builder, building the temple and a palace for himself and many fortified cities to protect Israel's borders. However, the gap widened between those with wealth and those in need. He used forced labour for building, which caused resentment, and after his death there was rebellion.

Useful websites

- http://commons.wikimedia.org
  (search for King Solomon)
- www.textweek.com/art/solomon.htm
  (use the scripture index for other information)
- http://gardenofpraise.com/bibl16s.htm (slides)

Younger pupils

You will need

* A velvet or rich-looking bag
* A small box of chocolates
* One person figure wearing a small paper crown
* Toy money
* Felt or paper dream cloud

Note: Be aware of nut allergies and make sure sweets are in date and safe for all children.

Questions
(See also page 11.)
* Why do you think the king chose wisdom?
* Why do you think God was pleased with the king?
* What would you ask for if given a choice of anything?

Script 1

Unpacking the bag

My bag is richly coloured, fit for a king.
There is a king in my bag, with a choice to make.
There are chocolates in my bag. I wonder what they are for.
There are coins in my bag, and a strange, strange dream.

The story

Our story takes place on a richly coloured cloth *(place cloth)*, for this is a story of a king *(add king)*. The king was tired *(yawn)*. He had just become king and wondered how he could rule his kingdom. The king went to sleep *(lay king down)* and dreamed *(add cloud)*. He dreamed that God *(sign 'God')* spoke to him and gave him a choice. He could choose anything he wanted.

The king thought about it *(sign 'think')*. He could choose to live a long time *(move hands apart)*. He could choose to be rich *(add some money)*. He could choose to get even with his enemies *(sign 'enemy')* or have everyone respect him *(salute)*. The king thought about it *(sign 'think')*. It was a difficult choice, harder than choosing a sweet from a box of chocolates when you like them all *(add chocolate box)*, but he had to choose.

The king thought some more *(sign 'think')*, and he chose wisdom *(sign 'wise')*, for wisdom would help him rule his people well. It would help him to know right from wrong. God *(sign 'God')* was pleased with the king's choice and gave him wisdom *(sign 'wise')*, as well as all the things he had not asked for—long life *(hands apart)*, money *(add more money)* and respect *(salute)*.

We may not have special dreams *(lift cloud)* and we may not be offered a choice of anything in the world *(indicate whole cloth)*, but we will have choices, and sometimes it will be more difficult than choosing chocolates from a box when we like them all. That's when we need wisdom.

Reproduced with permission from *More Bible Storybags*® published by BRF 2012 (978 1 84101 836 2) www.barnabasinschools.org.uk

THE CHOCOLATE BOX (SOLOMON'S WISDOM)

Script 2

Unpacking the bag

My bag is richly coloured, fit for a king.
There is a king in my bag, with a choice to make.
There are chocolates in my bag: red and purple, green, orange and one that is gold.
There are coins in my bag, and a strange, strange dream.

The story

You will need

* A velvet or rich-looking bag
* Five wrapped chocolates: one green, one purple, one red, one orange, one gold. Place them in a box. (You can substitute other colours and adjust the text, but make sure there is a gold one)
* One person figure wearing a small paper crown
* Felt or paper dream cloud
* Coins

Note: Be aware of nut allergies and make sure sweets are in date and safe for all children.

Our story takes place on a richly coloured cloth…	*Place cloth*
for this is the story of a king.	*Place king*
This is also the story of a choice.	
Like choosing one chocolate from a box…	*Place chocolate box*
to choose one is not to choose the others.	*Pick a chocolate and replace*
In the quiet of his room, the king slept.	*Place king on his side*
In his sleep he dreamed…	*Place cloud*
he was given a choice.	
He could ask for anything, but only one thing.	*Indicate one*
Like a hand hovering above chocolates in a box…	*Hover hand*
the king's mind went over the choices he could make.	
Should he choose riches?	*Add coins, pick orange sweet, replace*
Should he choose revenge on his enemies?	*Sign 'enemies', pick up red sweet, replace*
Should he choose long life…	*Extend hands, pick up purple sweet, replace*

Reproduced with permission from *More Bible Storybags®* published by BRF 2012 (978 1 84101 836 2) **www.barnabasinschools.org.uk**

THE CHOCOLATE BOX (SOLOMON'S WISDOM)

or the respect of everyone around?	*Salute, pick up green sweet, replace*
Still the king's mind was undecided.	*Hover hand*
Finally he chose.	
He did not choose riches.	*Pick up orange sweet, replace*
He did not choose revenge.	*Pick up red sweet, replace*
He did not choose long life…	*Pick up purple sweet, replace*
or the respect of everyone around.	*Pick up green sweet, replace*
He chose wisdom…	*Pick up gold sweet and place on cloth*
a hard one, one that most people left in the box.	
'Give me wisdom,' said the king…	*Sign 'wise'*
'that I may know how to do what is right to rule my people well.'	
So God gave him wisdom…	*Pick up gold sweet and place by king*
and, because he had chosen well, God gave him: riches…	*Pick up orange sweet and place by king*
and long life…	*Pick up purple sweet and place by king*
and the respect of everyone around.	*Pick up green sweet and place by king*
Life is often like a chocolate box.	*Lift box*
There are choices to be made.	*Show sweets*
To choose one thing…	*Lift chocolate*
is not to choose another.	*Replace*

Questions
(See also page 11.)
* In what ways is life like a box of chocolates?
* Is saying 'yes' to one thing also saying 'no' to something else?
* Why do you think the king chose wisdom?
* How do we get wisdom if it is not just given to us?

Reproduced with permission from *More Bible Storybags*® published by BRF 2012 (978 1 84101 836 2) www.barnabasinschools.org.uk

THE CHOCOLATE BOX (SOLOMON'S WISDOM)

The angry man

The story of Jonah

Using the storybag® in assembly

> ✂ **You will need**
> ✱ Some ready-primed pupils or staff

Introduce the assembly by learning the signs for the words 'God', 'sorry', 'forgiveness' and 'change'. Sign these words together. (See the list of signs on page 103.) Talk about when we might use these signs.

Today's story is about being sorry, change and forgiveness. Read the Bible story on page 102.

> **Comment**
> The story of Jonah is about a man who did not want to deliver a message to his enemies. Jonah knew that God would forgive them if they were sorry and changed—which is exactly what happened. Jonah would probably have been happier to have seen them punished. In the story, God is more willing to forgive than Jonah.
>
> It's easy to go through life being like Jonah, wanting others to get into trouble for their wrongdoing rather than wanting them to be sorry, to be forgiven and to change.

Reflection

Use the storybag® script 1 or 2 as a reflection. It can be read by the teacher, with pupils performing any gestures, sign language or sounds. Pupils can also hold up objects and people figures from the bag. PowerPoint visuals of the story cloths can be accessed via www. barnabasinschools.org.uk/cooling2.

Ask pupils to watch the signing of the words 'sorry', 'forgiveness' and 'change'. What do the signs tell us about their meaning? For example, 'forgiveness' and 'change' are similar. 'Sorry' is related to the heart (how we feel).

Prayer *(optional)*

Say or sign the key words in the following prayer.

God, you forgive us when we are sorry and truly want to change. Help us to pass on that forgiveness to others.

Using the storybag® in RE

Introduce the subject using some of the material from the assembly introduction (see page 101). On the same page you will find a comment on the biblical story. Select the appropriate script and turn to pages 9 and 10 to find ways of using it.

Biblical material

Jonah 1:1—4:11

The people of Nineveh were the enemies of Israel. One day, God told Jonah to go to the people of Nineveh with a message saying that they must stop their cruel ways. God would not ignore their cruel behaviour any longer.

'No way!' thought Jonah. 'They are not likely to believe me, and I know what God is like—he will be kind and forgive them, which will make me look a fool.' With that, Jonah got on a boat going in the opposite direction.

While Jonah was at sea, there was a terrible storm. The wind howled, the waves rose and the boat rocked. The sailors were scared. 'This is my fault,' said Jonah. 'It's because I won't go to Nineveh and tell the people to change. Throw me overboard and maybe the storm will stop.' The sailors did not want to throw Jonah into the sea but the storm just got worse, so they did as he said. Immediately, the sea calmed down. Jonah sank beneath the waves and was swallowed whole by a great fish.

In the belly of the fish, Jonah prayed and decided to do as God asked. The fish swam to the land and spat Jonah out. Jonah went to Nineveh and gave his enemies God's message and they believed him. They stopped being cruel and God forgave them.

'I told you so,' said Jonah to God. 'I knew you'd go all soft and forgive them.' With that, Jonah stormed off in a huff and sulked beneath a bush that shaded his head from the hot sun.

God sighed. Jonah had a lot to learn. God sent a worm to nibble the bush until it died. This made Jonah cross and upset, as the hot sun now beat down on his head, giving him a terrible headache.

'Jonah,' said God, 'you are cross and upset about a bush.'

'So I should be!' replied Jonah. 'I liked that bush. It kept me cool.'

'I liked and cared for those people,' said God. 'Isn't it right that I forgive them?'

Follow-up activities

Select from these activities, according to the age and aptitude of your pupils. (See also pages 11 and 12.)

1. Create a two-dimensional display of this story that reflects the layout of the bag. Add two-dimensional versions of items from the story. Place the appropriate story script and an open children's Bible on a table. Add questions and pupils' comments, and use them as a basis for discussion.

2. Make a big book of the story of Jonah. Start by reducing the story to basic sentences together as a class. Print the sentences and share them among groups. Each group can take charge of a page that they create around a sentence, adding more text, illustrations, comments and questions. Older pupils can make the book in groups for a younger class and create a fictitious example of a person today being sorry, changing and being forgiven.

3. Draw a series of storm clouds. The sailors and Jonah go through a 'storm of emotions'. On storm clouds, write what some of those emotions might have been. Add some thoughts that might have been going through their minds, drawing on the story for evidence. On some of the clouds, add beliefs about God that can be found in this story.

4. Interview a Christian about why they still read the story of Jonah today. Discuss the story first and prepare questions. If you cannot arrange an interview, use the 'email a believer' facility. Older pupils may wish to email a Jewish and Christian believer and compare their responses. (See http://pof.reonline.org.uk/emailproject/index.php.)

5. Look at the range of images and paintings of the Jonah story (see websites listed on page 103). Choose one that you think best represents the story, and say why.

6. Develop or incorporate the signs for 'sorry', 'change' and 'forgiveness' into a dance. Signs can be extended to whole body movements. The dance should express the meaning of these words.

Symbols used in the story

- Storm, fish and worm: symbols of the power of God the Creator.

Signs used in the story (British Sign Language)

- 'Sad': right hand held vertically in front of the face, side on. Move downward to just below the chin.
- 'God': hand at shoulder height, index finger pointing upwards, others curled inwards.
- 'Sorry': circle right fist on chest.
- 'Forgive': right palm open, touch mouth, then circle on the left hand in an anti-clockwise direction.
- 'Change': both fists face each other, swivel fists around each other.
- Prayer as a conversation with God: palms together in prayer, then open them like a book and move palms up and down.

Useful websites

- www.christiansigns.org.uk (search the 'vocab' section for the words 'prayer', 'God' and 'forgiveness')
- www.signstation.org (go to the BSL dictionary, then A–Z for the words 'sorry' and 'change')
- www.britishsignlanguage.com (for the word 'sad')

Reflective activity

Throughout the day, pupils can use the signs as appropriate and think about the way in which the actions reflect the meanings.

Assessment

Assess the pupils' understanding by observing them replaying the script, or ask them to talk about the display or write about it.

Background information and understanding the story

- Nineveh was the capital of Assyria (modern northern Iraq). The Assyrians were the enemies of Israel. It appears that Jonah did not want to take God's message to them as he feared they would repent and God would forgive them. Maybe Jonah was worried about feeling a fool if he warned them and then nothing happened because they repented. Jonah sailed to the farthest point in the Mediterranean, probably Spain—the opposite direction to Nineveh.
- The story is set in the eighth century BC. Christians are divided on how they understand this story. Some take it as historical truth; others see it as a parable about forgiveness built around a kernel of history.
- In the story, the people in Nineveh are described as sinful and cruel. In the story, God does not ignore wrong but he is willing to forgive—more willing than Jonah is. This story is read by Jewish believers at Yom Kippur, The Day of Atonement, when people think about wrongdoing, saying sorry and forgiveness. In the Bible, being sorry is not enough; repentance is being sorry plus making a change of direction in life.
- God is described in the story as working through nature—wind, storm, worm and fish (not a whale).

Useful websites

- http://gardenofpraise.com/bibl22s.htm (online jigsaw puzzle of Jonah)
- www.textweek.com/art/jonah.htm (use the scripture index for other information)
- www.biblical-art.com/biblicalsubject2.asp?id_biblicalsubject=20

You will need

* A dark blue bag
* Five people figures (Jonah, two enemies and two sailors)
* A worm (paper or felt)
* A big fish (paper or felt, big enough to cover Jonah)
* A boat (cardboard box with a card boat shape stuck on the side)
* Large bush (scrunched-up tissue paper)
* Yellow card sun

Questions

(See also page 11.)

* Why do you think the man did not want to take God's message to his enemies?
* Why do you think the man got in a temper when his enemies were sorry and God forgave them?
* Was forgiveness right?

Script 1

Unpacking the bag

My bag is storm-coloured.
There is a man in my bag who ran away.
There is a fish in my bag, and a worm that wiggles and nibbles.
There are people in my bag—some enemies and some sailors in their boat.
There is a bush in my bag that gives shade from the burning sun.

The story

Our story takes place on a deep blue cloth *(place cloth)*, for this is a story of a storm at sea. There is a boat on the sea *(add boat)* and sailors in the boat *(add two sailors)*, and a man who ran away *(add Jonah)*. Suddenly the wind grows wild and strong *(wind noises)* and the boat begins to rock *(rock boat)*. The waves rise high *(bunch cloth)* and all the people pray *(hands in prayer)*.

'This is my fault,' says the man who ran. 'God *(sign 'God')* asked me to go to my enemies and tell them to stop being cruel. I said no *(shake head)* and I ran away to sea *(undulate hand)*. Throw me overboard.' The sailors look sad *(sign 'sad')*. They don't want to do that, but when the storm grows worse *(bunch cloth)*, they do as he says and the man sinks down in the sea *(throw Jonah overboard)*.

God sees the man fall and sends a great fish to swallow him whole *(place fish over Jonah)*. Inside the belly of the fish, the man prays *(hands in prayer)*. In heaven, God *(sign 'God')* listens and sends the great fish to spit the man out on to dry land *(move fish and dump Jonah just off the bag)*.

The man walks to his enemies *(add enemies and walk Jonah to meet them)* and tells them to change—to stop being cruel, to stop being bad. The enemies listen. They say sorry *(sign 'sorry')* and decide to change *(sign 'change')*. God *(sign 'God')* in heaven forgives *(sign 'forgive')*.

'I told you so!' says the man, in a temper *(lift man and bang him down)*. 'I knew you would be soft. I knew you would forgive them *(sign 'forgive')*. That's why I ran away.' The man storms off and sulks under a bush *(add bush)*, which shades his head from the hot, hot sun *(add sun)*.

In heaven, God *(sign 'God')* sighs and whispers to a worm *(place worm)*. The worm wiggles and nibbles, nibbles and wiggles until the bush dies *(wiggle worm around bush, squash bush)*. The sun beats down on the cross man's head *(hand on head)*. He gets so hot, he wishes he were dead. God above *(sign 'God')* sighs *(sigh)* and quietly whispers, 'You are upset about a bush that kept you cool, an ordinary bush that died in the night. I felt for a people that were sorry *(sign 'sorry')* for their wrong. Isn't forgiveness *(sign 'forgive')* right?'

Reproduced with permission from *More Bible Storybags*® published by BRF 2012 (978 1 84101 836 2) www.barnabasinschools.org.uk

THE ANGRY MAN (THE STORY OF JONAH)

Script 2

Unpacking the bag

My bag is storm-coloured.
There is a man in my bag who runs away to sea.
There is a fish in my bag, and a worm that wiggles and nibbles.
There people in my bag—some enemies and some sailors in their boat.
There is a bush in my bag that gives shade from the scorching sun.
There's a whistle in my bag. I wonder what it's for.

You will need

* A dark blue bag
* Five people figures (Jonah, two enemies and two sailors
* A worm (paper or felt)
* A big fish (paper or felt, big enough to cover Jonah)
* A boat (the base of a cardboard box with a card boat shape stuck on the side)
* Large bush (scrunched-up tissue paper)
* Yellow card sun
* A whistle (if you cannot whistle)

The story

Our story takes place on a sea-storm cloth…	*Place cloth*
for this is a story of storms.	
Before the storm, all was quiet and an angry man sat in the shelter of a bush.	*Place bush and Jonah*
Then the one above called him…	*Sign 'God'*
to go to his enemies, far, far away…	*Indicate far away*
to speak to his enemies, far, far away…	*Indicate far away*
and tell them to change their sinful, cruel ways.	
'No!' thought the angry man…	*Lift Jonah and bang down*
'I know what will happen. They will repent and you will forgive.	*Sign 'forgive'*
Why should I care?	*Remove Jonah*
I will not go!'	*Remove bush*
The man found a boat going far, far away…	*Place boat and sailors*
far, far away in the opposite direction.	*Place Jonah in boat*
The one sighed and whistled up a storm…	*Sign 'God', sigh, whistle*
which whirled round the boat and whipped up the waves.	*Wind sounds*
The waves rose up and boat swung violently…	*Bunch cloth, rock boat*
and all the sailors prayed.	*Sign 'prayer'*

Reproduced with permission from *More Bible Storybags*® published by BRF 2012 (978 1 84101 836 2) www.barnabasinschools.org.uk

'This is my fault,' said the angry man.	*Lift Jonah*
'Throw me overboard into the sea.'	
The sailors went through a storm of emotions, but fearfully, tearfully, they did as he said.	*Drop Jonah overboard*
Sinking through the sea, the man faced his end, but a great fish came and swallowed him whole.	*Cover Jonah with fish*
Deep in the fish, the angry man prayed…	*Sign 'prayer'*
and the one above heard with a sigh of relief.	*Sign 'God', sigh*
The fish swam on till it came to the shore…	*Move fish and Jonah*
and it spat the man out on to dry land.	*Place Jonah on edge of cloth, remove fish*
The man walked on to the land of his enemies.	*Walk round cloth, place enemies*
He told them to change their cruel, sinful ways.	
The people believed him, and they were sorry…	*Sign 'sorry'*
and the one above forgave.	*Sign 'God' or 'forgive'*
'I told you so!' said the angry man and he stormed off to sulk beneath a bush.	*Move Jonah, add bush*
The one sighed and whistled to a worm…	*Sign 'God', sigh, whistle*
who wiggled and nibbled, nibbled and wiggled…	*Wiggle worm round bush*
until the bush died.	*Flatten bush*
The sun beat down on the angry man's head.	*Add sun*
He got so hot, he wished he were dead.	
The one sighed and whispered gently…	*Sign 'God', sigh heavily*
'You're upset about a bush that kept you cool, an ordinary bush that died in the night.	
I was upset for a people that were sorry for their wrong…	*Sign 'sorry'*
Which of us is right?'	

Questions

(See also page 11.)

* What sort of storms are there in the story?
* Who is the one above?
* What do you think is the answer to the last question in the story?

Reproduced with permission from *More Bible Storybags*® published by BRF 2012 (978 1 84101 836 2) **www.barnabasinschools.org.uk**

THE ANGRY MAN (THE STORY OF JONAH)

Pray and prey

Daniel in the lions' den

Using the storybag® in assembly

✂ You will need
* No props are needed

Introduce the assembly by making some rules and asking pupils why they are wrong or unfair. For example, say, 'The new rule is that anyone wearing long socks has to stay in at playtime. The new rule is that anyone who goes to Beavers or Rainbows is not allowed to sit down in assembly.'

Today's story is about prayer and a very unfair rule or law. Read the Bible story on page 108. See also www.refuel.org.uk/projects/ks1_topics/old_testament/old_testament.html.

> **Comment**
> Daniel carried on praying even when the king made an unjust law. He believed it was right to pray to God. Sometimes people work to get laws changed if those laws are unfair.

Reflection

Use the storybag® script 1 or 2 as a reflection. It can be read by the teacher, with pupils performing any gestures, sign language or sounds. (If you use script 2, you will need to explain the difference between 'prey' and 'pray'.) Pupils can also hold up objects and people figures from the bag. PowerPoint visuals of the story cloths can be accessed via www.barnabasinschools.org.uk/cooling2.

 Prayer *(optional)*

God who made the lion and the lamb and gave us a sense of justice, help us to be strong as lions for justice, but gentle as lambs in achieving it.

Introduce the subject using some of the material from the assembly introduction (see page 107). On the same page you will find a comment on the biblical story. Select the appropriate script and turn to pages 9 and 10 to find ways of using it.

Biblical material

Daniel 6:1–23

Daniel was an important man: he helped to rule the country for King Darius. Of all the king's helpers, Daniel was the brightest and the best, honest and hardworking. This made some people jealous. They tried to find fault with Daniel, but he was so honest that they gave up. Instead they came up with a plan to get rid of him.

Daniel's enemies went to the king and asked the king to make a law saying that no one was to pray to anyone but the king for 30 days. Anyone who prayed to God would be thrown to the lions. They knew that Daniel prayed to God three times a day and they knew he would not stop.

They were right. Daniel went on praying and his enemies told the king. The king realised he had been tricked and tried to save Daniel, but the law could not be changed. Daniel was thrown into the lions' den and the den was closed and sealed. King Darius wouldn't eat and couldn't sleep for worrying about Daniel. Would God save him?

In the morning, Daniel came out of the den unharmed. God's angel had shut the lions' mouths and he was safe.

Follow-up activities

Select from the activities below, according to the age and aptitude of your pupils. (See also pages 11 and 12.)

1. Create a two-dimensional display of this story that reflects the layout of the bag. Add two-dimensional versions of items from the story. Place the appropriate story script and an open children's Bible on a table. Add questions and pupils' comments, and use them as a basis for discussion.

2. Create a soundscape to accompany a retelling of the Bible story. The instruments should reflect the mood and events of the story in the sounds they create. Your soundscape could be used in an assembly.

3. Create a script for a puppet version of the play that will communicate what is important about the story. With younger pupils, create sentences for the puppets to say. A further option would be to photograph the puppet play (with permission) to create a PowerPoint retelling of the story. Create a final slide to say why Christians and Jewish believers still read this story today. Slides can also be printed and speech added.

4. Explore the lives of people such as Martin Luther King, who opposed unjust laws. In what ways was Martin Luther King like Daniel?

5. Show pupils a range of images of Daniel in the lions' den. Go to http://commons.wikimedia.org/ and search 'Daniel in the lions' den' for a range of copyright-friendly images. Ask pupils to give them points on a scale of one to three, depending on how much they like them. Discuss the results and ask for reasons. Repeat this with different questions—for example, 'Which image is the best at showing how Daniel felt? Which picture is best at showing the importance of prayer in the story?' Create a range of questions and use them to stimulate discussion.

6. Turn the story into a dance-drama with an interpretive narration.

Signs used in the story (British Sign Language)

- 'God': right index finger pointing upwards at shoulder height, other digits curled inwards.
- 'Sad': right hand held vertically in front of the face, side on. Move downward to just below the chin.
- 'Eat: right hand, fingertips touch thumb and tap lips.
- 'Enemy': bang sides of little fingers together, other digits curled inwards.
- 'Hate': right and left hands in fists. Place right fist above left fist and squeeze both independently.
- Prayer as a conversation with God: palms together in prayer, then open them like a book and move palms up and down.

Useful websites

- www.christiansigns.org.uk (search the 'vocab' section for the words 'prayer' and 'God')
- www.signstation.org (go to the BSL dictionary, then A–Z for the words 'eat', 'enemy' and 'hate')
- www.britishsignlanguage.com (for the word 'sad')

Reflective activity

Discuss what the BSL sign for 'prayer' conveys about prayer. Pupils can devise their own sign for the word 'prey' to communicate its meaning.

Assessment

Assess the pupils' understanding by observing them replaying the script, or ask them to talk about the display or write about it.

Background information and understanding the story

- ⚙ In the story, Daniel ignores a law that he considers wrong and suffers for it. For Christians, the laws of a nation should be obeyed as long as they do not ask people to do wrong.
- ⚙ Daniel is described as living within the Persian empire. The identity of Darius is uncertain, but he was possibly a king of part of the Persian empire (see http://bibleencyclopedia.com/darius.htm).
- ⚙ Daniel was one of many Jewish people who had been deported years before, to the area now known as Iran and Iraq.

Useful websites

- ⚙ www.biblical-art.com/biblicalsubject2.asp?id_biblicalsubject=19 (art for Daniel)
- ⚙ www.textweek.com/art/daniel.htm (use the scripture index for other information)
- ⚙ http://commons.wikimedia.org (search for 'lion and lamb')

Younger pupils

You will need

* A purple cloth bag
* A soft toy lion (child-safe)
* Four people figures (Daniel, king with crown and two enemies)

Questions

(See also page 11.)

* Why were the enemies jealous?
* Was the man right to ignore the new law?
* How do you think the king felt when he found he had been tricked?
* I wonder what prayer was said at the end.

Script 1

Unpacking the bag

My bag is a colour worn by kings.
There is a king in my bag, and a man who helps him rule.
There are enemies in my bag who hate the man.
There is a lion in my bag, a hungry lion.

The story

Our story takes place on a royal cloth *(place cloth)*, for this is a story about a man *(place Daniel)* who served a king *(add king)*. The man *(hold up Daniel)* was clever and wise, honest and good, but other people *(place enemies)* were jealous because he did his job well and was popular with the king. These people were his enemies *(sign 'enemy')*.

Every day, the man walked to his window and talked to God in prayer *(move Daniel, sign 'prayer')*. Day in, day out, the man prayed three times a day *(indicate three fingers)*. The enemies made a plan *(sign 'enemy')*. They went to the king *(move enemies to king)* and asked him to make a law that, for 30 days, people could only pray *(sign 'prayer')* to the king. Anyone who prayed to God would be thrown into a den of lions *(place lion at a distance and roar)*.

The man heard about the law, went to his window and prayed to God *(sign 'prayer')*. The enemies watched the man *(move enemies near Daniel)*, then went to the king *(move enemies)* and told him what had happened. The king was sad *(sign 'sad')* because he liked the man *(lift Daniel)*, and the man was his best helper, but the law could not be changed. The man was thrown into the lions' den *(move Daniel to lion, roar)*.

All night the king worried. He could not sleep *(tilt head to rest on hands, then lift head and shake it to indicate 'no')* and he would not eat *(sign 'eat', shake head)*. The next day, the king went to the lions' den *(move king to lion)* and found the man alive *(move Daniel to king)*. Then a different prayer was said *(sign 'prayer')*.

Reproduced with permission from *More Bible Storybags*® published by BRF 2012 (978 1 84101 836 2) www.barnabasinschools.org.uk

PRAY AND PREY (DANIEL IN THE LIONS' DEN)

Script 2

NB: in order to understand this script, pupils will need to know the difference between the words 'prey' and 'pray'. Improvise scenarios of animals of prey.

Unpacking the bag

My bag is a colour worn by kings.
There is a king in my bag, and a man who helps him rule.
There are enemies in my bag who hate the man.
There is a lion in my bag, and a gentle lamb.

Note: The lamb is kept off the cloth, just lifted at certain points.

You will need
* A purple cloth bag
* Soft toy lion and lamb (child-safe)
* Four people figures (Daniel, king with crown and two enemies)

The story

Our story takes place on a cloth fit for a king...	*Place bag*
for this is a story of a man who served a king...	*Place Daniel and king*
a man who prayed.	*Sign' prayer'*
The man who prayed was busy.	*Move Daniel about*
He was always busy...	*Move Daniel about*
doing this to rule, that to govern, much to do for the king.	
He stopped for a moment. In the distance he heard the lions roar...	*Hold up lion, pupils roar*
The lions were circling their prey.	*Place lion, make claws*
The man walked to his window...	*Move Daniel*
lifted his hands to heaven, and prayed...	*Sign 'prayer'*
to the one who made the lion and the lamb.	*Sign 'God', hold up lion and lamb*
He finished his prayers, and once again heard the distant roar of lions.	*Roar, lift lion*
The man had enemies.	*Place enemies round Daniel*
They too were circling...	*Circle them*
and he was their prey.	*Make claws*

PRAY AND PREY (DANIEL IN THE LIONS' DEN)

Older pupils

Questions
(See also page 11.)

* The man had done no wrong, so why did some people dislike him?

* Can a person be prey?

* How do the words 'pray' and 'prey' help us to understand this story?

They hated him…	*Sign 'hate'*
hated his power…	*Sign 'hate'*
hated his honesty…	*Sign 'hate'*
hated his friendship with the king.	*Sign 'hate'*
The enemies circled the king with wicked words…	*Circle enemies round king*
until he made a law that stopped all prayer, except to the king…	*Sign 'prayer'*
on pain of death.	
The enemies were laughing now.	*Draw smile in the air*
They would trap the man who prayed.	
Far away, the man heard the laughter and knew what it meant.	
He walked to the window…	*Move Daniel*
and raised his hands in prayer…	*Sign 'prayer'*
to the one who made the lion and lamb.	*Sign 'God', hold up lion and lamb*
The sound of circling lions was closer now.	*Circle lion, roar*
The enemies had him in their grasp.	*Pick up Daniel in fist*
They took him to the king…	*Put Daniel down near king*
who knew, too late, he had been tricked.	
The man stood in the circle of lions…	*Circle lion round Daniel*
still as a stone, silent and calm.	
Around him, great beasts moved on padded feet.	
From the centre of the circle, he prayed to the one…	*Sign 'prayer'*
who made the lion and the lamb…	*Hold up lion and lamb*
and angels' wings stopped the lions' mouths…	*Finger on lips*
who sat, gentle as lambs…	*Hold up lamb*
and all was silence.	*Shh… finger on lips*

Reproduced with permission from *More Bible Storybags®* published by BRF 2012 (978 1 84101 836 2) www.barnabasinschools.org.uk

PRAY AND PREY (DANIEL IN THE LIONS' DEN)

For such a time as this

Esther saves her people

✂ You will need
* A paper crown

Prayer *(optional)*

Lord, we may not be kings and queens. We may not be rich or powerful, but there are situations where help is in our power. Help us to see those situations and act.

Introduce the assembly with images of kings and queens or ask pupils what a king or queen does. Ask pupils to wear the crown for a few seconds and say one thing they would do if they were king or queen.

Today's story is about a queen who used her position to save her people. Read the Bible story on page 114.

Comment

This is a story about a girl who became a queen. She used her power and influence to help others. She did not want to help to begin with, because she was frightened, but she discovered that wearing a crown is not just about enjoying the power and riches; it's about helping others.

Each of us is king or queen in our little world, even if it is a world of one—ourselves. We may not rule over a kingdom, but we can rule over ourselves and use what we have to help others.

Reflection

Use the storybag® script 1 or 2 as a reflection. It can be read by the teacher, with pupils performing any gestures, sign language or sounds. Pupils can also hold up objects and people figures from the bag. PowerPoint visuals of the story cloths can be accessed via www.barnabasinschools.org.uk/cooling2.

Using the storybag® in RE

Introduce the subject using some of the material from the assembly introduction (see page 113). On the same page you will find a comment on the biblical story. Select the appropriate script and turn to pages 9 and 10 to find ways of using it.

Biblical material

Esther 1:1—8:17

Esther was a Jewish girl who lived long ago in the land of Persia. Her name means 'star'. Esther lived with her uncle, for she had no mother and no father. Esther grew into a beautiful woman and one day the king of Persia noticed her. The king chose Esther to be his queen and she moved into the palace. Her uncle never forgot her; he sat outside the palace and kept watch. He listened for anything that might bring danger.

The prime minister of Persia, Haman, hated the Jewish people and he plotted to get rid of them. Esther's uncle heard of Haman's wicked plan and he warned her: 'Maybe you became queen for such a time as this, for now you can help your people. Speak to the king and stop Haman.' Esther was frightened. No one, not even the queen, was allowed to go to the king unless the king asked them to come. What should she do? To go to the king without waiting to be called could lead to her death, unless the king held out the golden wand (sceptre). Only then would she be safe.

Esther asked her uncle to get all of her people to pray and said she would do the same. After several days, Esther put on her best clothes and got ready to go to the king. She entered the great hall and slowly walked towards the king. The king had not asked her to come and looked surprised, then he held out the golden sceptre and Esther breathed a sigh of relief. She was safe. Esther told the king about Haman's wicked plot. The king was furious. Haman was arrested and the Jewish people were saved.

Follow-up activities

Select from the activities below, according to the age and aptitude of your pupils. (See also pages 11 and 12.)

1. Create a two-dimensional display of this story that reflects the layout of the bag. Add two-dimensional versions of items from the story. Place the appropriate story script and an open children's Bible on a table. Add questions and pupils' comments, and use them as a basis for discussion.

2. In what ways was Esther a star? Write about Esther the star on a star template. In what ways can we be stars that shine for others?

3. Write some qualities that are weapons in the daily battle to live well today—for example, patience and self-control. Draw a sword and write your words for living well on the sword. Your words should be the types of qualities that allow good people to flourish.

4. Investigate the Jewish festival of Purim and how it relates to this story. Make links between the way the festival is celebrated and this story. People still celebrate the story after more than 2000 years. Why do you think people still celebrate it? Does it have a message for today? (See websites listed on page 115.)

5. Turn the word image of 'love as a web' into a visual image—for example, a sparkling web with words such as 'kindness' on it. Write an explanation of the image. Create your own word images for key parts of the story—for example, 'Courage like a...'

6. Esther saw her power as an opportunity to help her people. Look at appropriate people of power and influence today. How do they use their power and influence for others? How could they use their power and influence for others differently? How can we help others, using what influence we have?

Signs used in the story (British Sign Language)

- ✪ 'Courage' or 'brave': right hand, fingers curled slightly inwards. Pull fingers away from chin in this position.
- ✪ 'Sad': right hand held vertically in front of the face, side on. Move downward to just below the chin.
- ✪ 'Beauty': right hand, all finger tips touching the thumb tip. Touch lips and open hand as you remove it.
- ✪ 'Love': arms crossed with palms flat to the chest, then move away from chest and uncross.
- ✪ 'Mother': tap right palm on right side of the head.
- ✪ 'Father': tap right index and middle finger over left index and middle finger.
- ✪ Prayer as a conversation with God: palms together in prayer, then open them like a book and move palms up and down.

Useful websites

- www.christiansigns.org.uk (search the 'vocab' section for the word 'prayer')
- www.signstation.org (go to the BSL dictionary, then A–Z for the words 'mother', 'father', 'beauty', 'love' and 'brave')
- www.britishsignlanguage.com (for the word 'sad')

Reflective activity

Make a web from wool. An adult can hold the ball while pupils stand in a circle and hold the thread as it is passed across the circle to them. Talk about creating webs of love around people.

Assessment

Assess the pupils' understanding by observing them replaying the script, or ask them to talk about the display or write about it.

Background information and understanding the story

- The king in this story may have been Xerxes I (486–465BC). The name Esther is Persian and means 'star'. Her Jewish name was Hadassah.
- When Esther heard about Haman's plot, she fasted for three days, which means that she went without food or reduced her food. Fasting was usually accompanied by prayer.
- In 721BC, many Jewish people had been taken to Assyria (northern Iraq), when the Assyrian empire conquered northern Israel. Later, in 586BC, many more people had been carried off to Babylon (southern Iraq), when the Babylonians took over from the Assyrians. Finally, in 539BC, the Persians defeated the Babylonians and once again the Jewish people changed masters. Persia is the modern Iran.
- The constant deportations left Jewish people scattered throughout the Middle East. The Persian emperor, Cyrus, allowed the Jewish people to go home and rebuild their temple, but some families, like Esther's, decided to stay. The record of this policy of returning deported peoples is written on the Cyrus cylinder in the British Museum (see www.britishmuseum.org/explore/highlights/highlight_objects/me/c/cyrus_cylinder.aspx).

Useful websites

- www.textweek.com/art/esther.htm (use the scripture index for more information)
- www.holidays.net/purim (Purim celebrates Esther's story)
- www.torahtots.com/holidays/purim/purim.htm (children's Purim activities)

You will need
* A gold bag
* Five people (small Esther, adult Esther, king, uncle, Haman)
* Two small silver card crowns
* Small queenly cloak
* A small roll of gold paper for the wand (to fit the king)
* A star sticker or shape

Questions
(See also page 11.)
* Why was Star frightened?
* What did Star do when she was frightened?
* Why do you think she asked everyone to pray?

Script 1

Unpacking the bag

My bag is gold for a king and queen, and these are the crowns they wear.
There is a girl in my bag who grows, and an uncle who cares for her.
There is a cloak in my bag, fit for a queen.
There is a golden sceptre in my bag, a special royal wand,
a star for a star, and an enemy.

The story

Our story takes place on a golden cloth, for this is the story of a king and queen *(place cloth, add crowns)*. In the land of Persia, long ago, lived a little Hebrew girl whose name means 'star', with no mother and no father *(place small Esther)*. But Star was loved *(sign 'love')* and her uncle looked after her as his own *(place uncle)*.

Star grew up and became a beautiful woman, as lovely as a star *(replace small Esther with adult)*. The king *(place king, add crown)* was looking for a queen. He chose Star and she moved to the palace *(place crown on Esther, move her and king)*. Her uncle followed *(move uncle)* and sat outside, keeping watch for any danger. One day he heard *(cup ear)* that the wicked prime minister, Haman, was planning to kill all their people *(add Haman)*. The uncle warned Star and told her to act *(move Esther to uncle)*. 'Maybe this is why God helped you to be queen. Now you can help your people,' said her uncle.

Star was frightened, but she listened to her uncle *(cup ear)* and said she would help *(move Esther to be on her own)*. Star prayed *(sign 'prayer')* and asked all her people to do the same. For three days *(three fingers)* they prayed *(sign 'prayer')*. Star put on her best clothes *(add cloak)* to go to the king. She knew this was dangerous, for no one *(shake head)*, not even the queen, could go to the king unless he asked her to come. Only if the king held out the golden wand *(place wand by king)* would she be safe.

Star walked down the hall *(walk her slowly)*, and the king held out the golden wand *(hold up wand)*. She was safe! Star told the king of the prime minister's wicked plans *(lift Haman)* and he was arrested *(remove Haman)*. Star had saved her people. She was a real star *(add sticker)*!

Reproduced with permission from *More Bible Storybags®* published by BRF 2012 (978 1 84101 836 2) www.barnabasinschools.org.uk

FOR SUCH A TIME AS THIS (ESTHER SAVES HER PEOPLE)

Script 2

> NB: The story uses a number of British Sign Language signs. You may wish to teach the signs first so that pupils can join in.

Unpacking the bag

My bag is gold for a king and queen, and these are the crowns they wear.
There is wool that weaves a web and scissors to cut it.
There is a child in the bag who grows into a beautiful woman.

The story

You will need

* A gold bag
* Some red wool and some blue wool
* Small child-safe scissors
* Two small silver card crowns
* Three people figures (small Esther, adult Esther, king)

Our story takes place on a golden cloth…	*Place cloth*
for this is the story of a king and queen.	*Place crowns*
For such a time as this, a star was born.	*Place small Esther*
But what sort of time was this?	*All make a question mark in the air*
A sad time…	*Sign 'sad'*
for a young girl without a mother or father…	*Sign 'mother' and 'father'*
but her people wove a web of kindness around her.	*Circle of blue wool*
They brought her up secure and loved.	*Sign 'love'*
For such a time as this, the little girl grew in faith and courage.	*Sign 'God' and 'brave'*
But what sort of time was this?	*All make a question mark in the air*
An ordinary time, a time of growing up…	*Indicate growing with hands*
within a web of kindness…	*Lift blue wool, replace*
for the girl without a mother and father.	*Sign 'mother' and 'father'*
For such a time as this, the little girl grew into a woman.	*Replace small Esther with adult figure*
But what sort of time was this?	*All make a question mark in the air*

Reproduced with permission from *More Bible Storybags*® published by BRF 2012 (978 1 84101 836 2) www.barnabasinschools.org.uk

FOR SUCH A TIME AS THIS (ESTHER SAVES HER PEOPLE)

An exciting time, for the woman became a great beauty…	*Sign 'beauty'*
was noticed by a king…	*Place king, add crown*
and became the queen.	*Move Esther to king, add crown*
For such a time as this, the woman was a queen…	*Move king and queen*
and lived in a palace.	*Move Esther on alone*
But what sort of time was this?	*All make a question mark in the air*

A dangerous time.

An enemy wove a web of danger round her…	*Circle red wool round Esther*

and around her people.

For such a time as this was…

the love…	*Sign 'love'*
the faith and courage…	*Sign 'God' and 'courage'*
the beauty…	*Sign 'beauty'*
the power of being 'queen'.	*Touch crown*

She took her weapons in her hands…

drew on her courage and prayed…	*Sign 'brave' and 'prayer'*
and called on those who loved her.	*Sign 'love'*
She cut the web of danger…	*Cut red wool*

and saved her people.

Questions

(See also page 11.)

* How can kindness be like a web that surrounds?
* In what ways could wickedness be like a web?
* How can love, faith, beauty and courage be described as weapons?

Reproduced with permission from *More Bible Storybags*® published by BRF 2012 (978 1 84101 836 2) www.barnabasinschools.org.uk

FOR SUCH A TIME AS THIS (ESTHER SAVES HER PEOPLE)

Enjoyed
this book?

Write a review—we'd love to hear what you think. Email: reviews@brf.org.uk

Keep up to date—receive details of our new books as they happen.
Sign up for email news and select your interest groups at:
www.brfonline.org.uk/findoutmore/

Follow us on Twitter @brfonline

By post—to receive new title information by post (UK only), complete the form below and post to: BRF Mailing Lists, 15 The Chambers, Vineyard, Abingdon, Oxfordshire, OX14 3FE

Your Details
Name _____
Address_____
_____
Town/City _____ Post Code _____
Email _____

Your Interest Groups (*Please tick as appropriate)

☐ Advent/Lent

☐ Bible Reading & Study

☐ Children's Books

☐ Discipleship

☐ Leadership

☐ Messy Church

☐ Pastoral

☐ Prayer & Spirituality

☐ Resources for Children's Church

☐ Resources for Schools

Support your local bookshop
Ask about their new title information schemes.